Origami Instruction Book for Kids Animals Edition

Fun and Easy Projects for Beginners and Adults Too

Ben Mikaelson

Table of Contents

Introduction 1
Chapter 1: All About Origami 3
Chapter 2: What You'll Need 5
Chapter 3: How to Make a Square from a Rectangle 7
Chapter 4: A Few Folds 9
Chapter 5: Symbols for Getting Started 18
Chapter 6: A Tiger (Face) 20
Chapter 7: Pig 27
Chapter 8: A Bulldog (Face) 32
Chapter 9: Fish 38
Chapter 10: Owl 44
Chapter 11: Bat 52
Chapter 12: Bear Cub 59
Chapter 13: Lion 69
Chapter 14: Penguin 78
Chapter 15: Platypus 84
Chapter 16: Gorilla 93
Chapter 17: Swan 103
Chapter 18: Giraffe 109
Chapter 19: Squirrel 116
See You Soon! 125

© Copyright 2018, All rights reserved.

The following eBook is reproduced below with the goal of providing information that is as accurate and reliable as possible. Regardless, purchasing this eBook can be seen as consent to the fact that both the publisher and the author of this book are in no way experts on the topics discussed within and that any recommendations or suggestions that are made herein are for entertainment purposes only. Professionals should be consulted as needed prior to undertaking any of the action endorsed herein.

This declaration is deemed fair and valid by both the American Bar Association and the Committee of Publishers Association and is legally binding throughout the United States.

Furthermore, the transmission, duplication, or reproduction of any of the following work including specific information will be considered an illegal act irrespective of if it is done electronically or in print. This extends to creating a secondary or tertiary copy of the work or a recorded copy and is only allowed with express written consent from the Publisher. All additional right reserved.

The information in the following pages is broadly considered a truthful and accurate account of facts and as such, any inattention, use, or misuse of the information in question by the reader will render any resulting actions solely under their purview. There are no scenarios in which the publisher or the original author of this work can be in any fashion deemed liable for any hardship or damages that may befall them after undertaking information described herein.

Additionally, the information in the following pages is intended only for informational purposes and should thus be thought of as universal. As befitting its nature, it is presented without assurance regarding its prolonged validity or interim quality. Trademarks that are mentioned are done without written consent and can in no way be considered an endorsement from the trademark holder.

Introduction

Congratulations on downloading *"Origami Instruction Book for Kids Animals Edition: Fun and Easy Projects for Beginners and Adults too."* You are about to embark on an incredible adventure! Perhaps you've already joined me in *"Origami for Kids: Easy Japanese Origami Instruction Book for Kids"* - this was the first book in the series. If not, don't worry! You'll find that this book is just as fun, and just as easy to follow along. The first book covered a variety of projects, while this book covers animals of all kinds. So, if you're a fan of origami and animals, this is certainly the book for you.

There is something very fun and special about taking a simple piece of paper and transforming it into something admirable. In this book, we'll be learning to make colorful, sweet, and even fierce animals (lions, tigers and bears, oh my!). You can make your favorites or make them all and have yourself your very own paper jungle. Whatever you decide, you'll find that each project here is easy to follow, beautiful, and most of all, fun! There are little hidden treasures throughout the book, like fun facts about Japan, and all kinds of cool things about our animal friends. Some of our buddies here are a bit more difficult to make, but if you're not an origami expert, don't worry! Just like in the first book of the series, these projects progress from easiest to the more difficult, so take your time and enjoy the adventure from the start. By the time you get to the end of the book, you'll certainly be an animal origami expert.

Coming up are some instructions (with pictures!) on the different folding symbols, and the different kinds of folds we will be making in our origami projects. You can look back to these sections if you happen to forget, or if you just need some extra help. You'll also be learning how to make a square sheet of paper from a rectangular one, so that you'll be able to use just about any kind of paper you have around the house. That means you'll have a larger variety of colors and patterns to choose from. Your animals are going to be amazing and certainly unique!

There are many books available about origami. I'm greatly appreciative you've chosen to join me for this one, thank you! I sincerely hope you enjoy reading and making each design here. If you find even one moment in which you're smiling, then my job is done. Share some happiness with friends and family by giving these projects as gifts, teaching someone else how to do origami, or even reading this book with others and learning to do origami together. It's a lot of fun to do with others! Are you ready to get started? I hope so! Here we go…

Chapter 1: All About Origami

Before we get to folding and creating our animal works-of-art, let's talk a bit about what origami is, and where it came from. Maybe this is your first time reading about origami. Maybe you've read about it before, like in the first book in this series: *Origami for Kids: Easy Japanese Origami Instruction Book for Kids*. Either way, it's good to brush up your knowledge and maybe even learn something new.

Origami (said like or-i-gah-me) is the Japanese work for paper folding. "Ori" means "to fold" and "gami" (kami in Japanese) means "paper". Put them together, and you have "origami" which is "to fold paper", of course. I know you already figured that out. Origami is an art form that has evolved and travelled through generations (from adults passed on to kids like you, and when those kids are all grown up, they pass it on to kids, and it just keeps going) throughout Japan. I know, you probably already knew that too. But what you may not know is that origami actually *started* in China, not Japan. Paper was *very* expensive back then, so only people with a lot of money used it, and some very wealthy emperors would practice origami as an art, and be given paper and origami as gifts.

After a while, paper became more affordable, and then everyone was using it for all kinds of things. Origami became more and more popular, mostly in Japan, and they really began to make some amazing things. Japan really made origami what it is today. Since that is where it evolved and gained popularity, even though it may have started in China, it's an important part of Japanese culture. Origami is usually taught at home as part of Japanese tradition.

Origami is more than just art...

So now you know where origami started and how it gained its popularity and spread to Japan. While there are beautiful, elaborate works of origami that are most certainly works of art, the benefits of origami don't stop there. It is actually very good for our mental and physical health.

Scientists have discovered that doing activities that challenge our mind and build on our existing abilities and talents through a variety of tasks, like puzzles and- you guessed it- origami, can strengthen the brain. Origami is an activity that can provide both mental and physical stimulus with a bit of exercise. Using the hands for direct contact activity helps stimulate certain areas of the brain. Origami helps build and strengthen hand-eye coordination, mental concentration, and fine motor skills. Paper folding is even used in therapeutic causes, like art therapy and stroke and injury rehabilitation.

Since origami has detailed instructions, it challenges us at a cognitive level as we learn to follow these instructions, obtain new skills, and complete new activities. When you engage in origami, impulses are sent to the brain that then begin activating both the left and right hemispheres. The tactile, motor and visual areas of the brain are activated and brought into use. This also stimulates the memory, non-verbal thinking, attention, 3D comprehension and imagination.

Origami also creates added emotional health. When we learn something new and create something (like any of these cool paper animals), we get a sense of satisfaction, pride, and other feel-good emotions. This helps boost creativity, self-esteem, and confidence. All these great things just from simple paper folding.

Chapter 2: What You'll Need

One of the things that makes Origami so special is that you don't need much at all. A simple piece of paper can be transformed, almost like magic, into something entirely new. Who knew that a piece of paper could become a giraffe, a squirrel, a fish, and so much more? I certainly didn't, until I learned all about this amazing art.

The first thing you'll need to get started is some square sheets of paper. Squares and rectangles look kind of alike, so how do you know which one is a square? That's a good question. When the paper is a square, all of the four sides will be the same length. A rectangle has four sides too, but two sides are longer than the other two. Take a look at the picture below, and you'll see what I mean. Just because a sheet of paper is a rectangle, though, doesn't mean you can't use it- you just have to make it into a square first. In just a minute, you'll learn how to do just that.

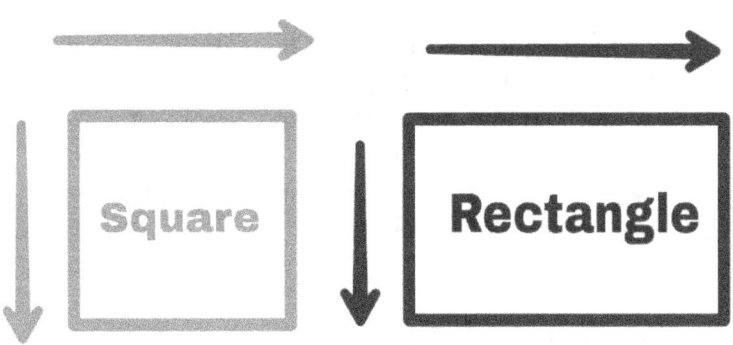

There are specially made papers for origami in all kinds of textures, colors, and patterns, but you really don't need anything fancy, especially to get started and practice. You probably have some paper around the house that is just perfect. Ask an adult to help you track some down if you need to. You can use whatever color or pattern you like. You can even use some plain white paper. Or take some white paper and color it yourself. This is especially nice to use for a gift, plus it adds some extra fun. You can use colorful pages from an old book (with permission, of course!), notebook paper, and lots of other things. Get creative! When you choose your paper, you don't want to use something too thick (like card stock or thick construction paper), because it is pretty hard to fold. You also don't want something too thin (like tissue or wrapping paper) because it tears very easily. Other than that, the sky is the limit, so get creative and go wild!

Once you have some paper, find a flat surface to work on. It doesn't have to be a desk; you can do origami just about anywhere. A coffee table or kitchen table are both great places, and of course a desk is also perfect. You just need a small area of a flat surface to fold on. Even a lap desk will work.

So, do you have your paper, and a place to fold it? Great! Now, some people like to use special tools to help make the folds *very* tight by pressing them down harder, but you don't need to worry about that. Just be sure to press down firmly when you make your folds.

The very last thing you need is maybe some patience. When you learn something new, you might make mistakes, or not understand right away. That's ok! I certainly didn't know these things when I was young, and now here I am making a book to teach you. Maybe you'll make your own book one day! Keep trying and practicing, and soon you'll find that you've got the hang of it. Remember to have patience for others that might be trying to learn with you as well.

Fun Fact: One pine tree can be made into about 80,500 sheets of paper. That's a whole lot of origami!

Chapter 3: How to Make a Square from a Rectangle

Remember when I said you could make a square from a rectangle? Now I'm going to show you how. For this, you *will* need a pair of scissors. If you need some help, ask an adult.

Take a look at the pictures below for each step to making a square. There are just 3 easy steps. First, lay your paper flat.

Step 1

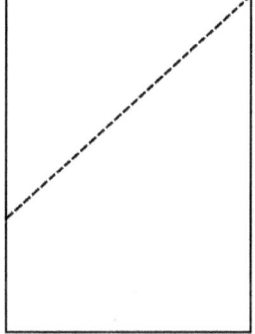

Fold #1: Fold along the dotted line, matching edge to edge.

Step 2

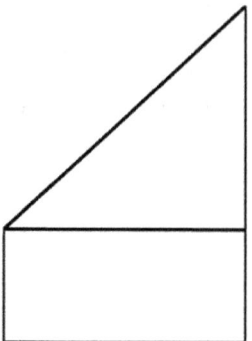

See the bottom section, away from the edge you folded down? Trim that off with your scissors.

Step 3

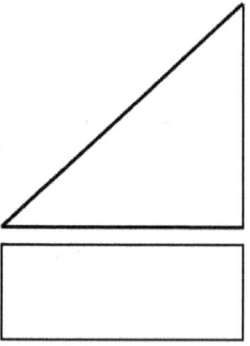

Unfold your paper, and you're done! Now you have a square to work with.

Chapter 4: A Few Folds

There are a few folds in some of these projects that are a little trickier than the basics. Now, you many already know these folds, but just in case, here's some extra help in case you need it. Let's start with the very basics, and work our way up.

Every piece of origami uses what we call a mountain fold, and/or a valley fold. You've made these many, many times with other projects that had nothing to do with origami- that's how common and easy they are.

The Valley Fold: Do you know what a valley is? It's a lower "dip" in the land, which is why this fold is called a valley. For a valley fold, the crease is made by folding the paper upward into itself, creating a "v" shape, or what looks like a "dip" in the paper. Take a look.

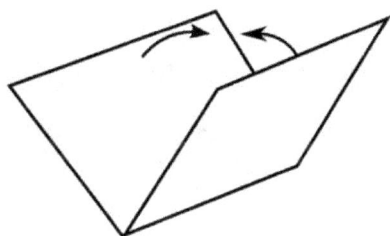

The Mountain Fold: Like a valley is low, a mountain is a high point or peak. The mountain fold is basically the opposite of the valley fold. For a mountain fold, the crease is made at the top, and the paper folded down on to itself, rather that up onto itself, formed and upside down "v". Here's how it looks:

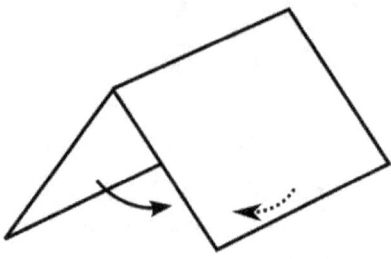

The Squash Fold: The squash fold is a rare one in this book. Only the two projects in this book involves the squash fold. At first it might look kind of hard, but once you understand, it's really not! You may have already done a squash fold before and just not realized what it was called. To make a squash fold, pry open the paper, and then flatten (or squash) it down. Take a look at the set of images below. These pictures show one example of a piece using a squash fold. Your first squash fold will be with the Bear Cub project, so when you get to it, refer back to this section if you need to.

Step 1

Lift the flap that is to be squashed up towards you.

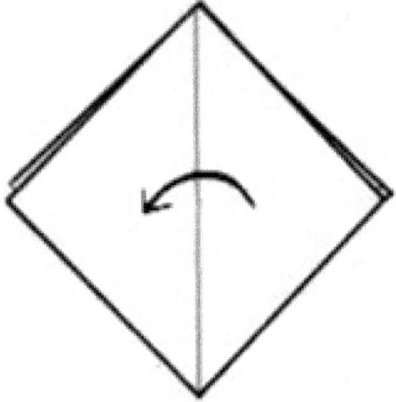

Step 2 and 3

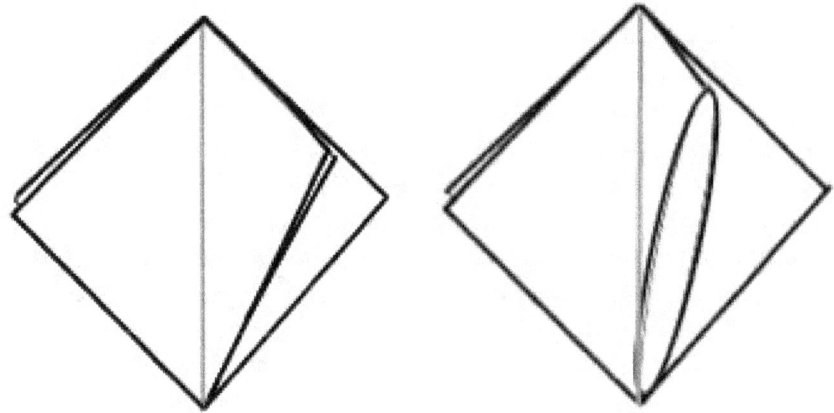

Separate apart the layers of paper.

Step 4 and 5

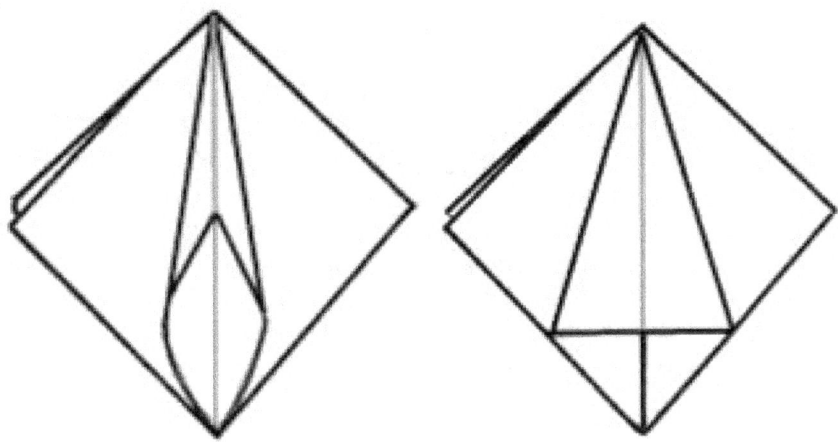

Carefully press down to squash the paper creating two new folds. Align the crease on the top layer of paper with the layers of paper beneath.

The pocket fold: The inside reverse fold, also called the pocket fold, is another common fold made in origami. To make this fold, follow the steps below. The pictures here are to help you understand how the fold works; we're not making anything here, really. We're just learning the different folds and practicing. You can come back to this section whenever you need to.

Step 1

Take a square piece of paper, and fold it in half, so that it looks like the picture below. Then fold along the dotted line, is indicated in the picture as well.

Step 2

The image below is what your paper should look like after step one. Now unfold, shown by the arrow.

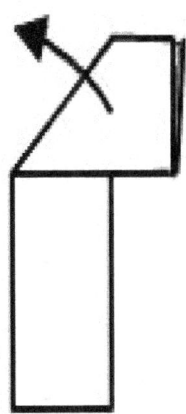

Step 3

See the large black arrow? Fold that corner inward and down along the dotted line, so that it is sandwiched on the inside, like a pocket.

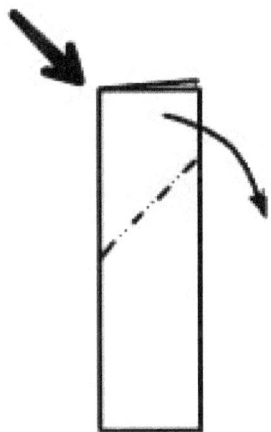

Step 4

The image below is what the final result should look like! Making a crease and then folding the paper to the inside is always the point of a pocket fold, which is what you just did.

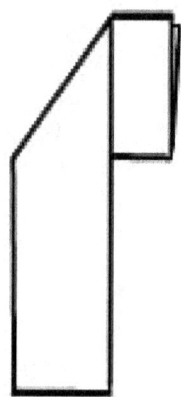

The hood fold: The outside reverse fold, also called the hood fold, is very similar to the pocket fold. Look at the images below to see the differences and similarities.

Step 1

This time, fold your paper in half from right to left. Then fold along the dotted line, as shown by the arrow in the picture below.

Step 2

Now unfold the previous step, as shown below again by the arrow.

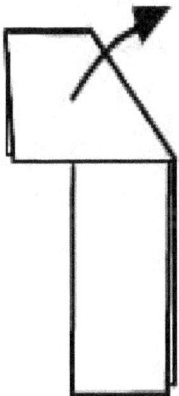

Step 3

Fold again along the dotted line shown below, but this time while opening the paper and pushing the lower half (the section below the dotted line) up and to the inside. Take a look at step 4 to see what I mean, and what it should look like.

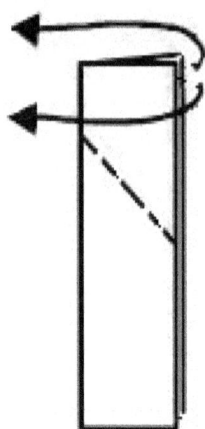

Step 4

This is what your paper should look like when you've completed step 3. Don't forget, you can always ask for help if you're having some trouble. You'll get it in no time!

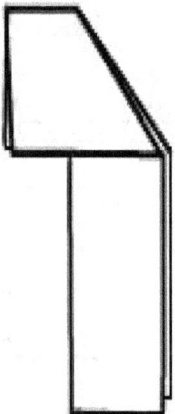

The Stair Fold: just like the other folds here, the stair fold is called that because it resembles the step of a stair. For this, we'll practice on a square piece of paper, just like what we use with all origami.

Step 1

Start with a mountain fold, folding a segment of the paper backwards, where the small dotted line is in the picture below. Turn the paper over (this isn't always required or possible with every origami project, but for learning the fold, it helps!).

Step 2

Using the same segment that you folded backward, make a fold where the thicker dotted line is in the picture below, and return the paper to its original position by turning it over.

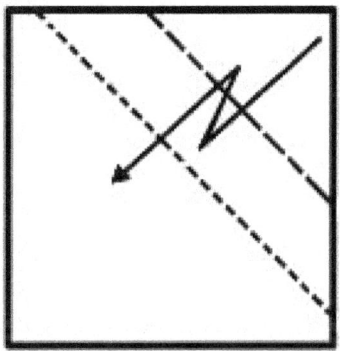 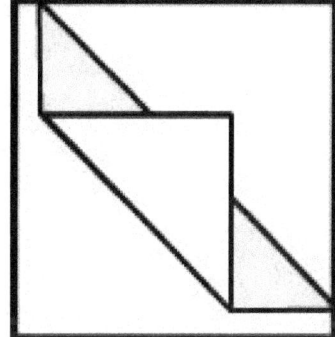

Chapter 5: Symbols for Getting Started

Each project in this book has written instructions as well as pictures to help you fold the very best you can. The pictures also have some special symbols to help you understand what's going on in the pictures. Before we get started on our very first animal friend, I'm going to show you each symbol you might see, and explain what they all mean. Don't worry, it's easier than it sounds!

Here's our first set of symbols:

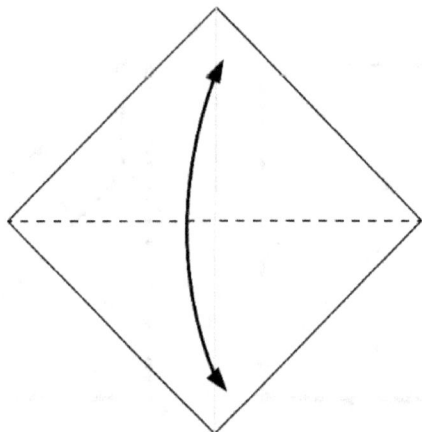

How many symbols do you think you see? There are three here. First, the dotted line in the middle from left to right. See it? A dotted line means this is where you **fold and unfold**. Now, see the solid gray line going from the top to the bottom? You have a good eye! This solid line shows you where the crease of your folds should be. Lastly in this picture, you see an arrow. The arrow shows you in which direction you need to fold.

Now let's look at the next symbol:

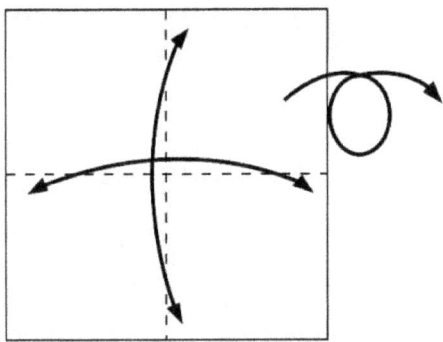

Here, you can see two sets of arrows. Do you remember what those mean? If you think it shows which direction to fold, you're right! Now, see the arrow with a loop? When you see this funny loopy arrow, it means you need to turn the paper to the other side.

There are more symbols to learn as you get better and better, but for now, this is all we need to know to start making adorable and ferocious animals. I hope you are as excited to learn as I am to teach you! Are you ready? Here we go!

Chapter 6: Tiger (Face)

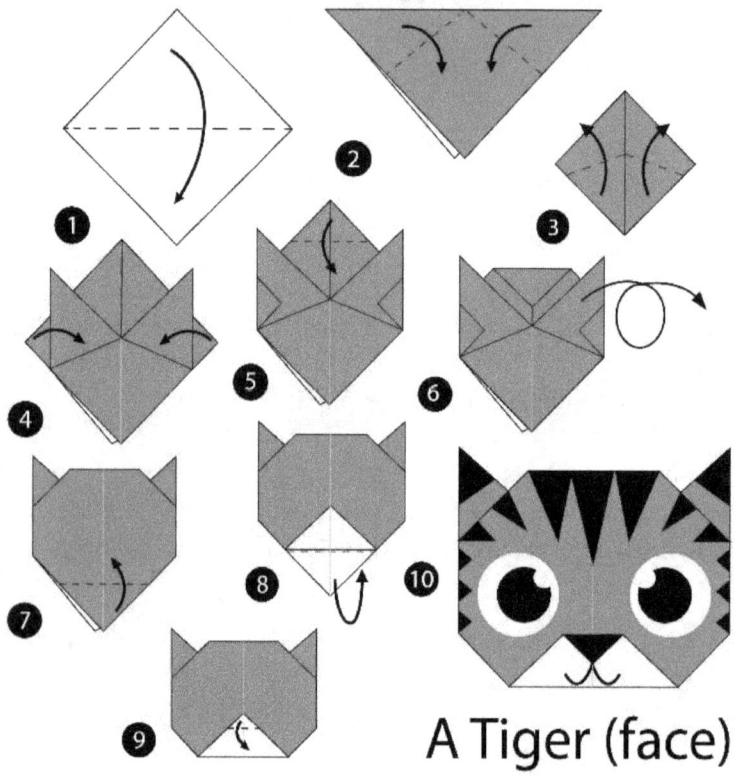

A Tiger (face)

This adorable tiger face is the very first origami project I remember doing! Start off with your paper flat on your work surface with the color or pattern side facing down. If you just have white paper that is fine too.

Step 1

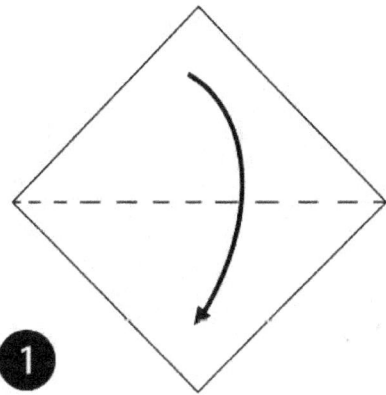

Fold in half from top to bottom, across the dotted lines.

Step 2

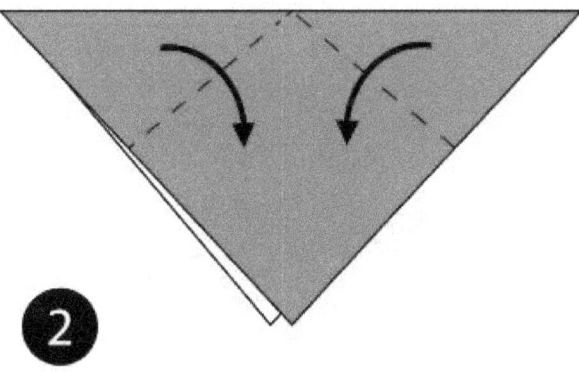

Fold the left point down to the center. Repeat this with the right point, so that they meet in the center. The folds will be where you see the dotted lines.

Step 3

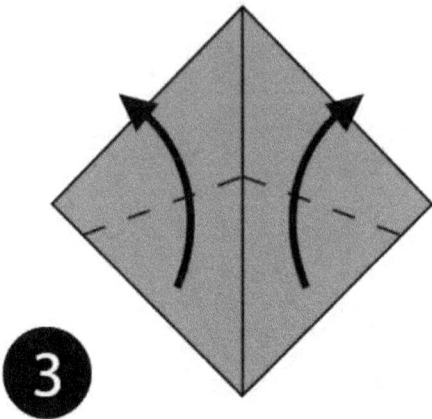

Fold the left point upwards and out a bit towards the left. Repeat this with the right point. You can see what it looks like by looking at the next picture.

Step 4

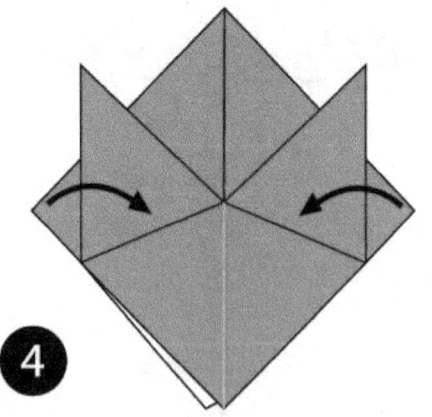

Fold the left point over as shown in the picture. Repeat with the right point. Be sure to crease well.

Step 5

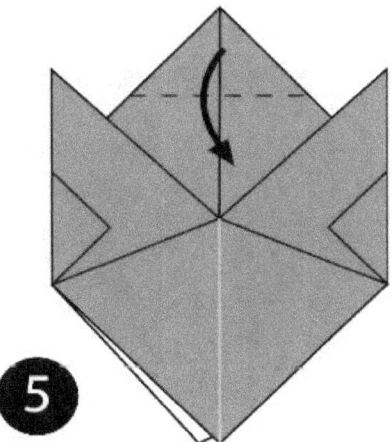

Fold the top point down, following along the dotted line. Crease well.

Step 6

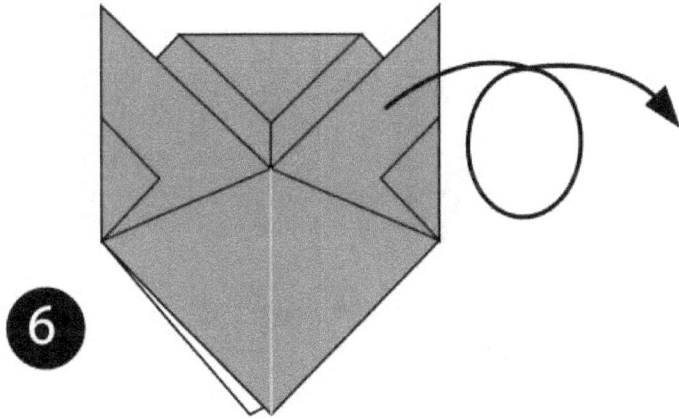

Turn the whole project over, like shown in the picture.

Step 7

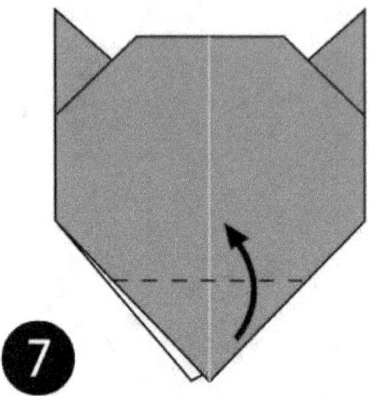

Fold just the top layer of paper (not both layers of paper) upward.

Step 8

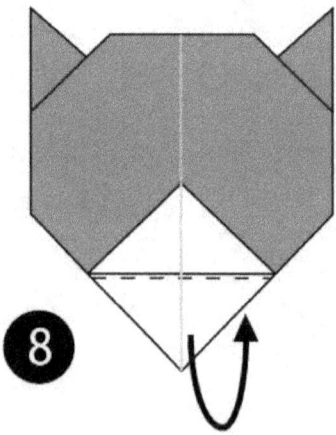

Now you have a point folded up with one layer, and one layer pointing down. Fold the point on the bottom backwards, behind everything. Crease well.

Step 9

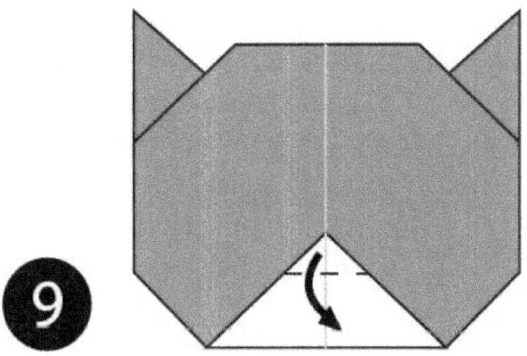

Now fold the tip of the point on top down as shown to make the tiger's nose.

Step 10

A Tiger (face)

You're done folding your tiger face! Now you can add your tiger's stripes, nose, and eyes. You can also decide that maybe this isn't a tiger after all, and color it as a jaguar, black panther, or a house cat.

Fun fact: The tiger is the biggest species of the cat family They can reach a length of up to 11 feet and weigh as much as 660 pounds. That's a big cat!

Did you know… the Japanese word "kami" for paper can also mean "spirit" or "god". This is because origami was originally used in spiritual or religious ceremonies. Nowadays, it's used for all kinds of things.

Chapter 7: Pig (Face)

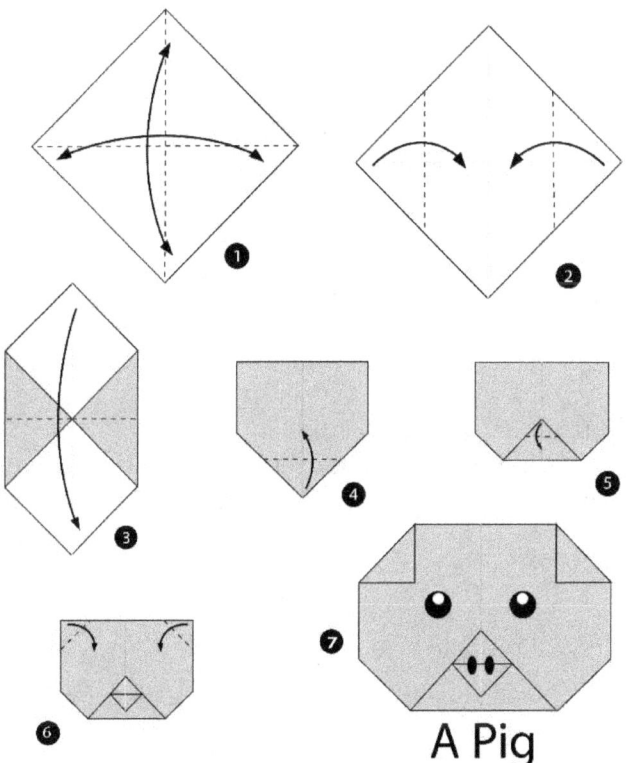

Oink! Oink! Here's another adorable animal face to add to your collection. Just like the tiger, this little piggy is super easy to make. Start with your paper flat on your work surface with the color or pattern side facing down, in the shape of a diamond.

Step 1

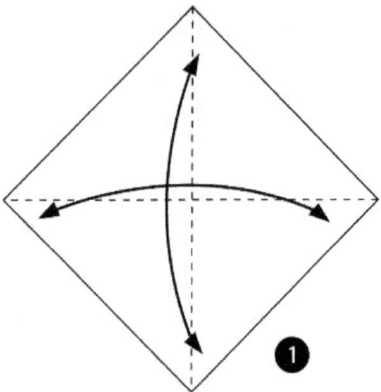

Fold the left corner straight across to the right one, as shown by the dotted line. Crease well, then unfold. *Fold #2:* Fold the bottom corner to the top, where the dotted lines are shown. Crease well and unfold again.

Step 2

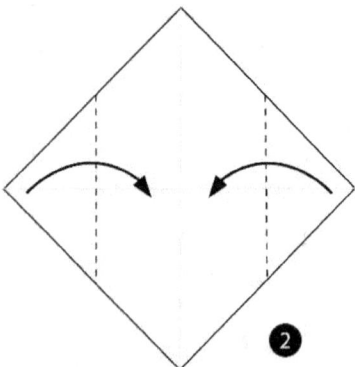

You should now have creases where the solid grey lines are shown in the picture. Fold the left corner over to the center, and crease well.

Now fold the right corner the same way, so that they meet in the center.

Step 3

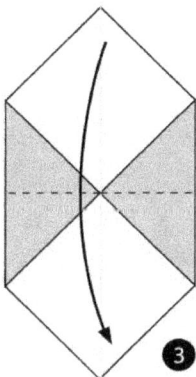

See the arrow in the picture? Fold the top point all the way down to the bottom point, as shown by the arrow. You're folding the project in half.

Step 4

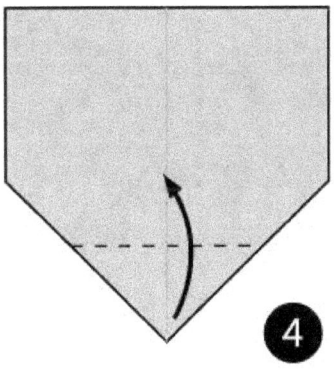

Fold the bottom point up as shown in the picture. Crease well.

Step 5

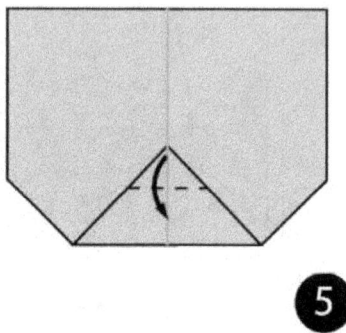

Fold the top point down, as shown in the picture. This is going to be your pig's snout.

Step 6

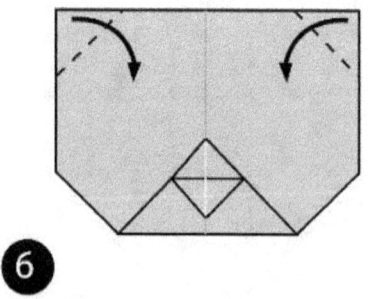

Fold along the dotted line on the left side as shown, and repeat the same thing on the right side. These are the ears.

Step 7

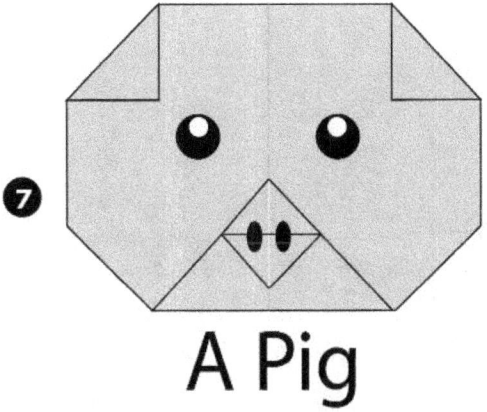

And you're done! Now you can give your pig's face some detail by drawing on its eyes and holes on its snout.

Fun Fact: Pigs are one of the most intelligent domesticated animals, even smarter than dogs!

Did you know… paper was first invented in China in 105 CE. It was first made from the hemp plant.

Chapter 8: Bulldog (Face)

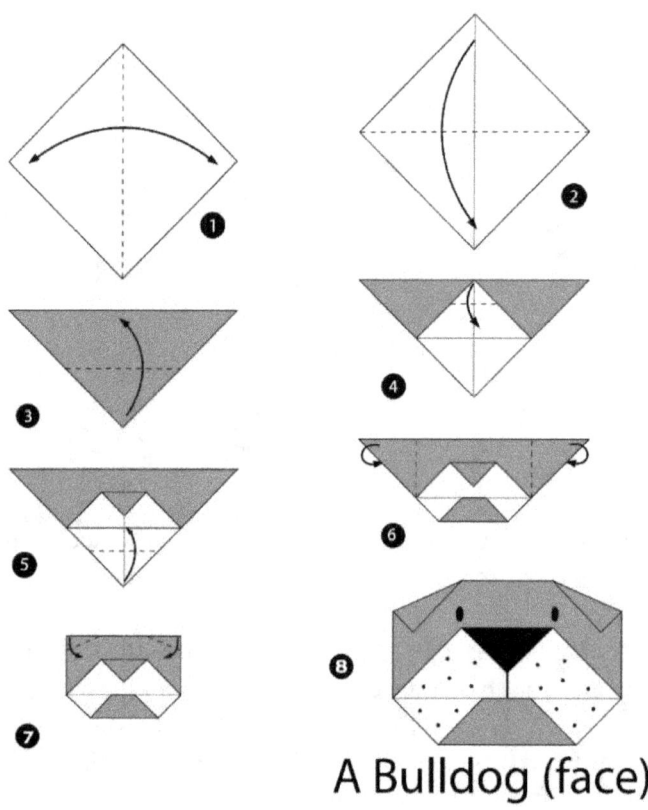

A Bulldog (face)

So far, we have a tiger, a pig and now it's time to add a dog into the mix! And what better dog to add than a bulldog? To make this cutie, start with your paper flat on your work surface with the color or pattern side facing down, and with the paper in the shape of a diamond.

Step 1

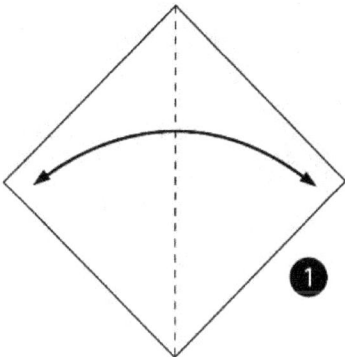

Fold your paper in half along the dotted line as shown, folding it in half from left to right. Crease well, then unfold.

Step 2

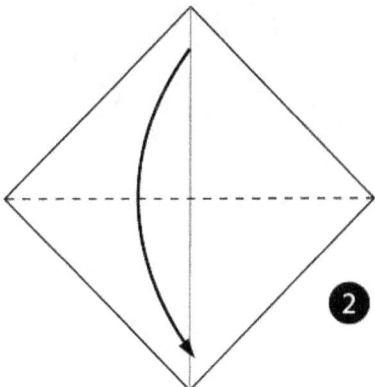

Just as you did in step one, you'll be folding the paper in half here again, but this time folding from top to bottom, as shown. Crease well, and this time leave it folded.

Step 3

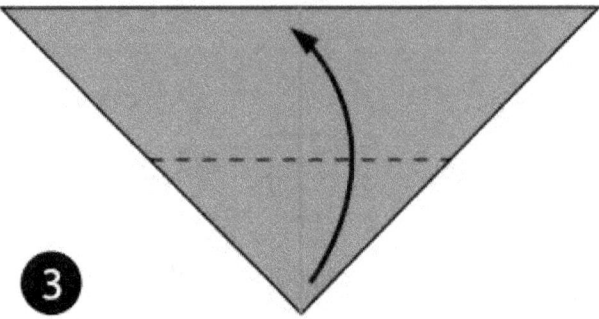

Fold the top layer of the bottom point up so that it touches the top edge. You can see what I mean by looking at the picture in step 4.

Step 4

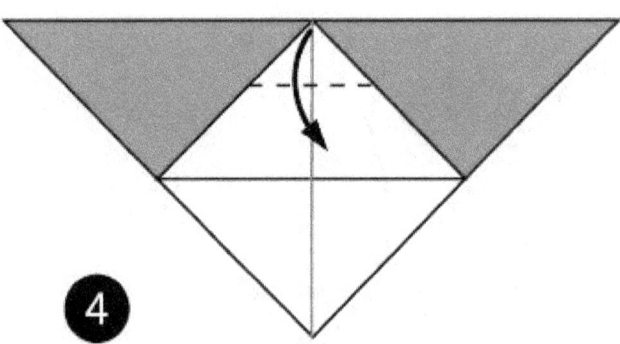

Now fold the top point to the center, as shown by the dotted line.

Step 5

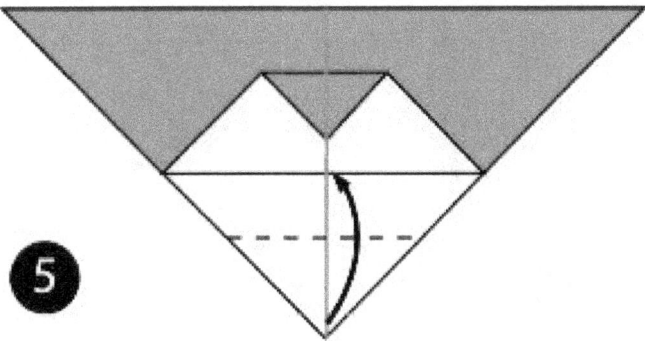

See the dotted line in this step? Fold the bottom point upward along the dotted line as shown, and crease well. And then tuck in a tiny portion of the paper like in the picture below.

Step 6

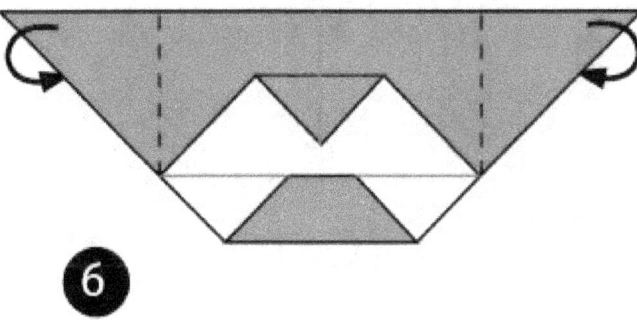

Fold backwards along the dotted line on the left side as shown. Then repeat this same fold on the right side, so that they match.

Step 7

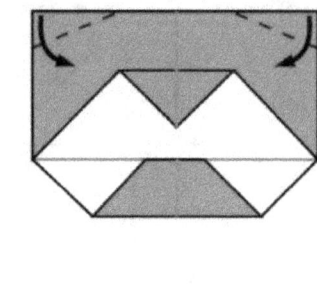

See the dotted lines on both sides? Fold down along them as shown in the picture.

Step 8

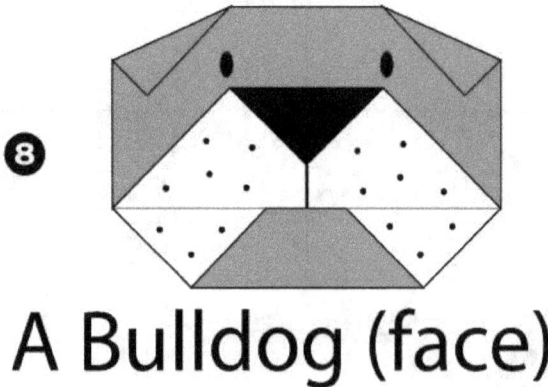

A Bulldog (face)

Your bulldog face is ready to have its features and details drawn on. How will your dog look? Maybe it has sleepy eyes, or ones that are wide awake. Does your dog have a black nose, or a pink one? Maybe it has spots!

Fun Fact: Bulldogs are courageous, loyal, and laid-back, which makes them great furry family members. They are good watch dogs, but also love being close to their family and cuddling.

Did you know… Origami has a strong link to math, and has been used in developing things such as airbags in cars.

Chapter 9: Fish

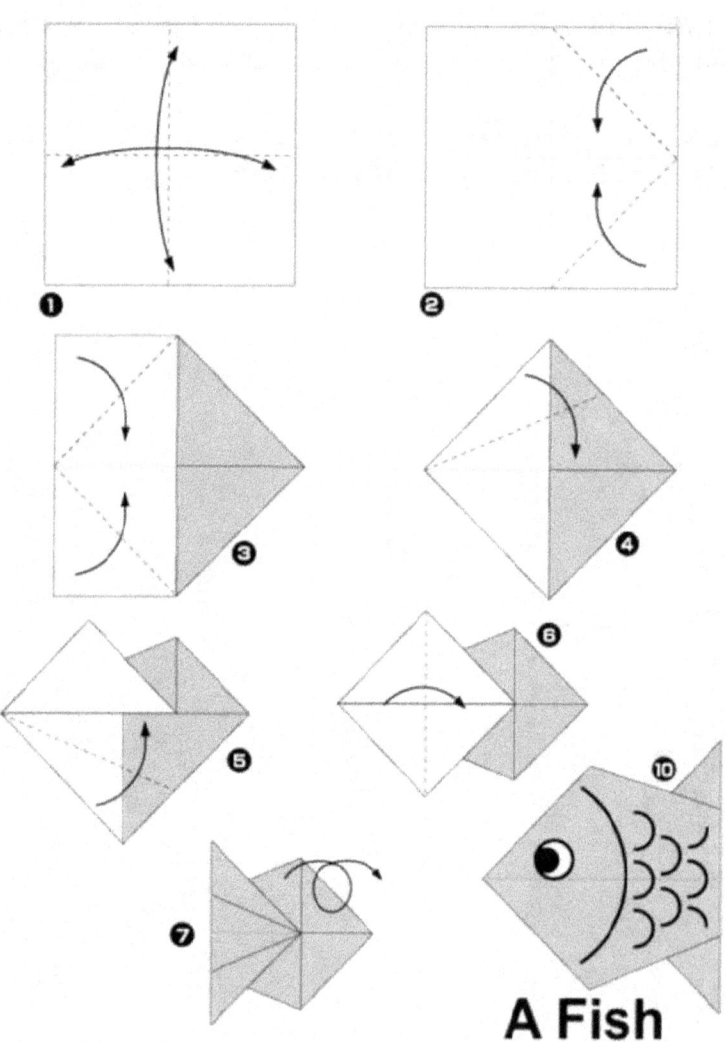

A Fish

Like most projects, start with your paper flat on your work surface, with the color (or pattern) side face down. The color or pattern will be the color of your fish. Position your paper so it is a square.

Step 1

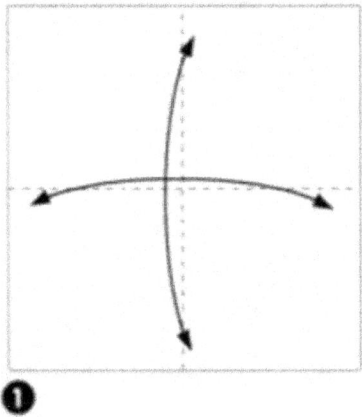

Fold in half from top to bottom, across the dotted lines. Crease well, and unfold. Now fold in half from left to right, crease well, and unfold again. This step is very easy, you're simply making two folds and then unfolding. This is your first step to creating your fish!

Step 2

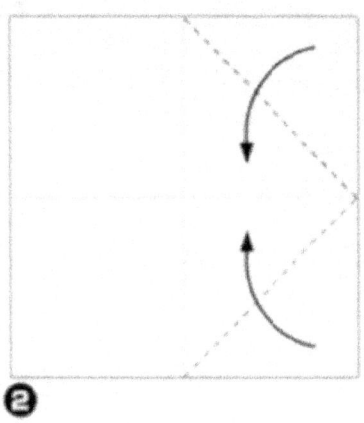

See the solid lines in the picture? You should now have a cross shape in the center of the paper where the creases were formed; these are shown with the grey lines. Fold the lower right corner up to the very center of the cross. Do the same with the upper right corner, by folding the upper right corner to the center as well.

Step 3

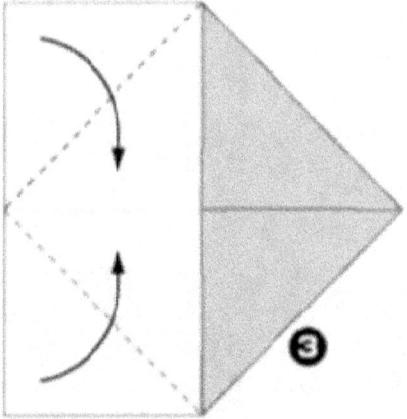

Repeat the third and fourth folds on the left side of the paper, as shown in the picture, but instead of folding them to meet in the front, fold them behind to the center of the cross on the back. Now you should have a folded square that is half one color, half another (if the front and back of your paper is different in color, of course).

Step 4

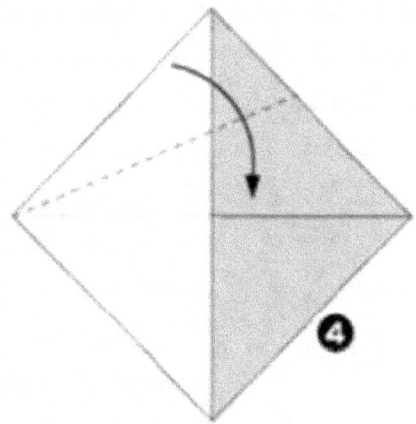

Following the arrow, fold across the dotted line making the edge meet in the middle. This will cause the portion you folded backwards to form a "flap" on the front.

Step 5

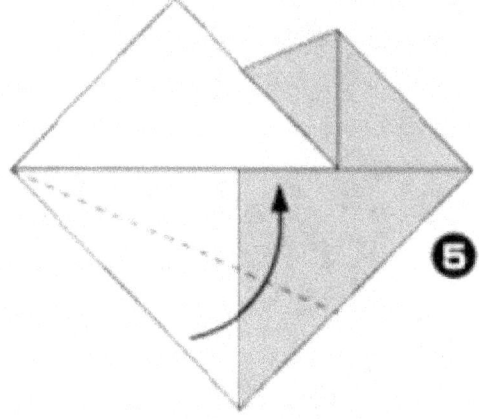

Repeat step four on the lower left side, as shown, by folding the lower corner up to the center, following the dotted line. This will be forming a second "flap". Both flaps together now form a square.

Step 6

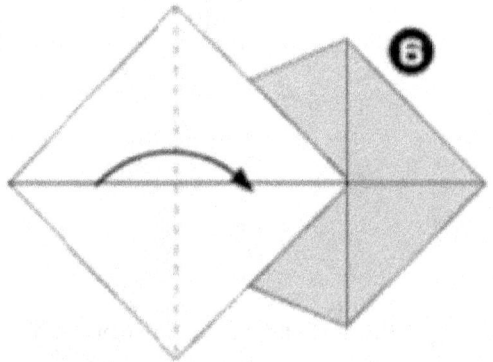

Now fold the left point of the square formed by the flaps over to meet the other point of the square.

Step 7

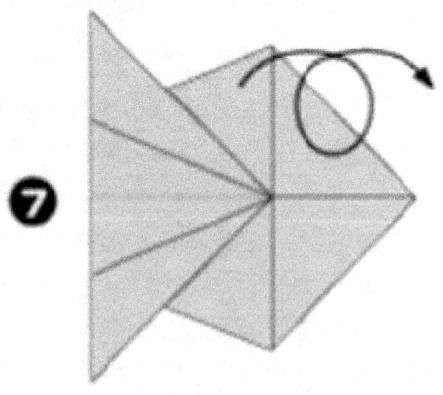

Turn the entire piece over.

Step 8

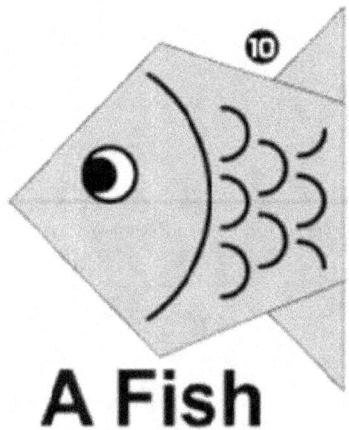

Ta-da! All done! You've made you're first origami fish! Now you can customize your fish to your liking. Maybe you can even make it some fish friends!

Fun fact: Fish have been around for more than 450 million years, even before the dinosaurs!

Did you know... The first book about origami was published in 1797. It was called 'Sembazuru Orikata' (Thousand Crane Folding), and it was written by Akisato Rito. Instead of paper folding instructions, the book talked about different cultural customs and traditions in Japan.

Chapter 10: Owl

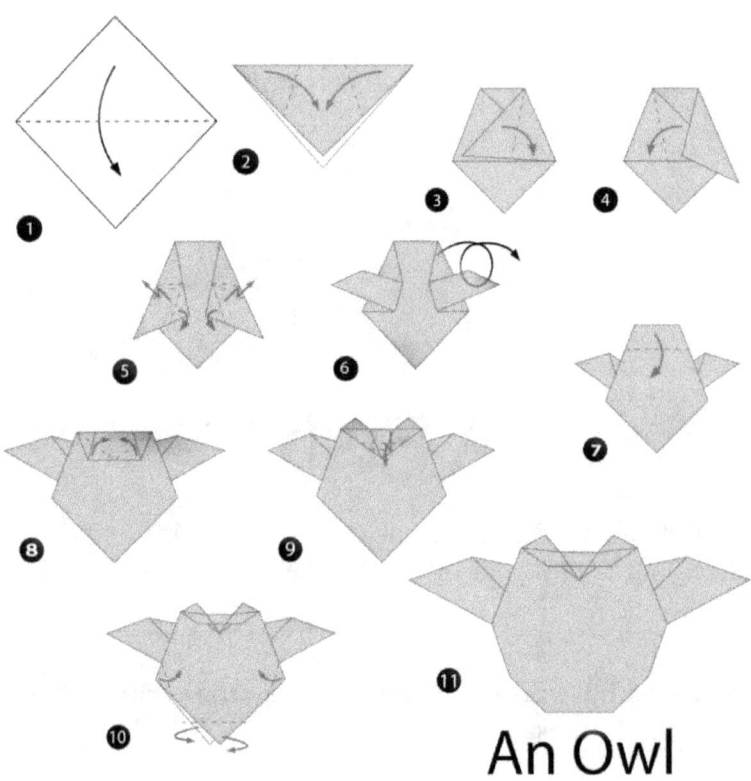

An Owl

Start with your paper flat on the surface, color (or pattern) side down, laying in the shape of a diamond. Just like our other animals, the color or pattern facing down will soon become the color of your owl's "feathers."

Step 1

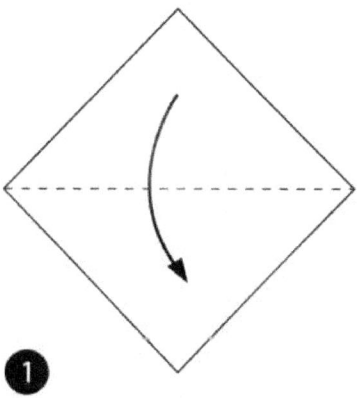

Fold your paper in half from the top to the bottom, as shown by the dotted line.

Step 2

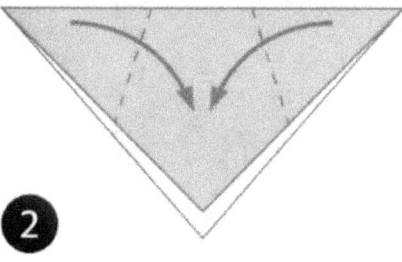

See the dotted lines and the arrows? Fold the left corner across so the tip touches the opposite edge, as shown in the picture below. Then do the same with the right corner, so they overlap in the center. Remember to crease well.

Step 3

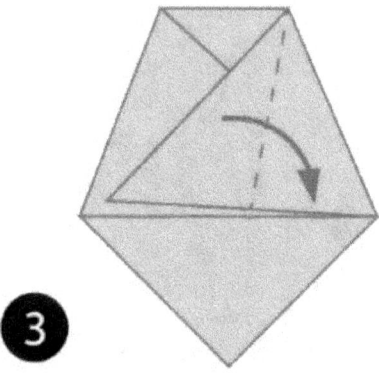

Fold back along the dotted line following the direction of the arrow, as shown in the picture. You can see what it should look like in step 4.

Step 4:

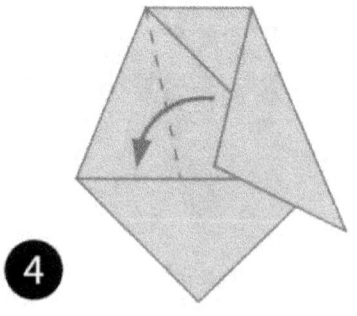

Just like in step three, fold the flap that's resting beneath the side you just folded by following the dotted lines again. These are your Owl's wings.

Step 5

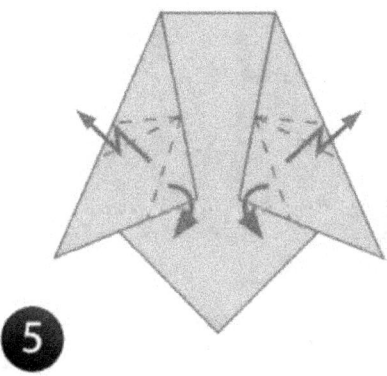

Now we need to finish the wings. Take a look at the dotted lines that are more towards the center of your piece, along with the two arrows in the center. Fold each point backwards and beneath the rest of the flaps. Crease well. Now see the remaining dotted lines with the zig-zag arrows on each side? Perform a stair fold on the left flap, and then repeat on the right side. You can look at the picture in step 6 to see what it should look like.

Step 6

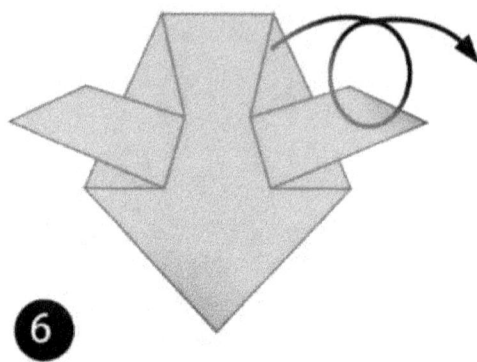

Ok, this isn't really a fold! Just turn the whole origami piece over. Super easy!

Step 7

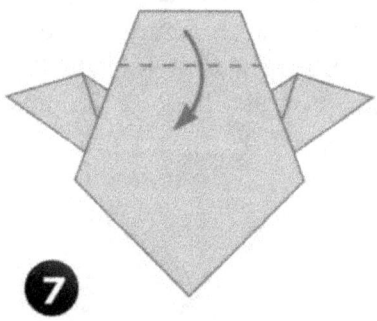

Fold the top down, as shown with the dotted line and arrow. Crease well here, we're making the owl's face!

Step 8

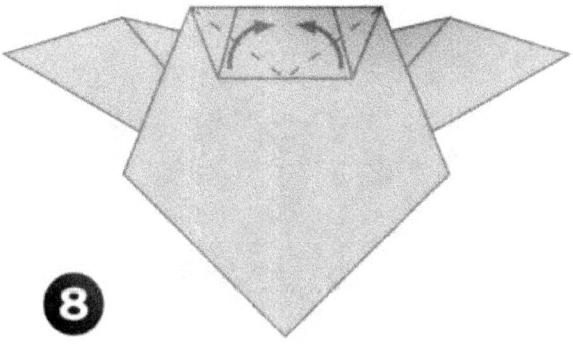

Follow the dotted lines on the left and fold the corner up so that it touches the top edge. Repeat this for the right side. Crease well.

Step 9

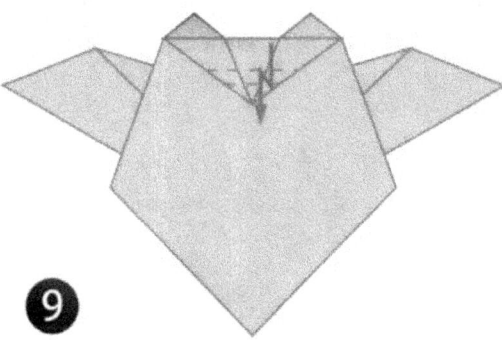

This might look a little tricky because it's on a small point, but it's really not. This is just a stair fold. Remember you can always refer back to the folds section towards the beginning of the book if you need to refresh your memory.

Step 10

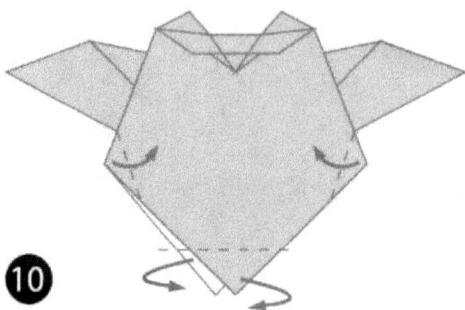

See the arrows at each corner on the side? Fold these two corners backwards along the dotted lines and crease well. Now, see how there are two layers of paper at the bottom? Fold the top layer backwards so that it's folded to the inside. Then fold the remaining bottom layer upward so that it's on the inside as well.

Step 11

An Owl

Ta-da! Your owl is now complete! You can add some texture lines in for feathers, or leave it as-is. Draw on some facial features, and decorate your owl however you like. Just have a hoot!

Fun fact: There are no owls in Antarctica! It's too cold, even for them. Can you think of some animals that *do* live in Antarctica? Are there any in this book?

Did you know... The Guinness Book of World Records has dozens of records regarding the craft of origami, like the object that has been made with the most folds, the smallest and the biggest objects, fastest time for folding 100 cranes, and more.

Chapter 11: Bat

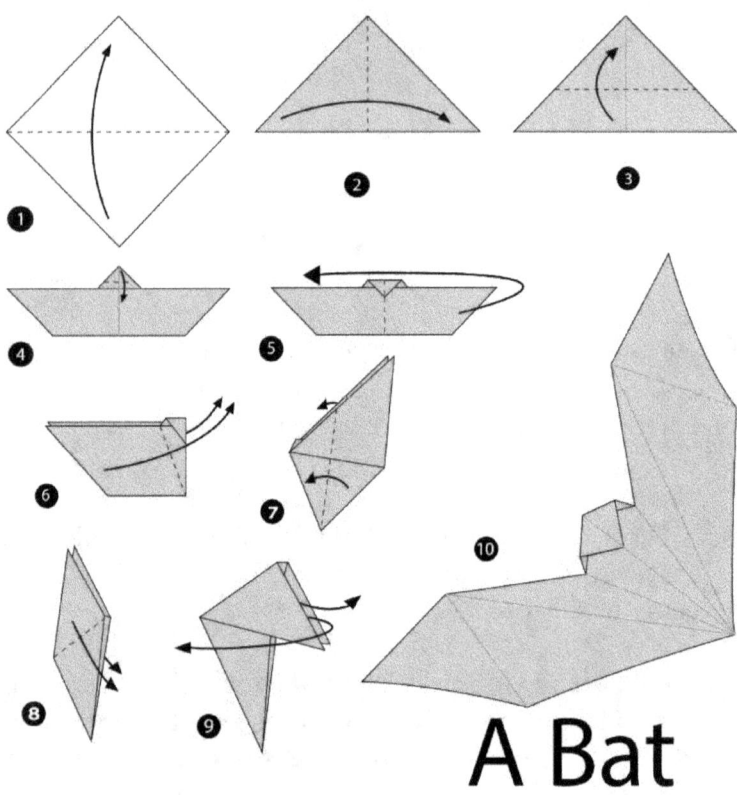

A Bat

Start with your square sheet of paper flat on your work surface with the color (or pattern) side facing down (this will be the outside, or "fur" color of your bat). Lay it down this way in the shape of a diamond (remember you can follow the picture instructions as well).

Step 1

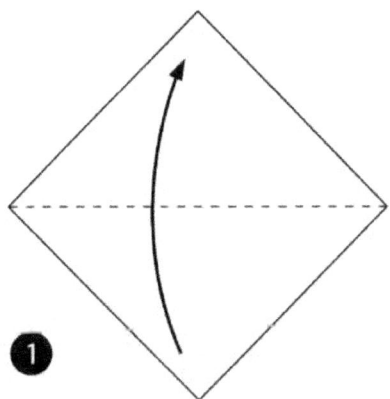

Fold your paper in half from the bottom corner to the top corner. You will now have a triangle.

Step 2

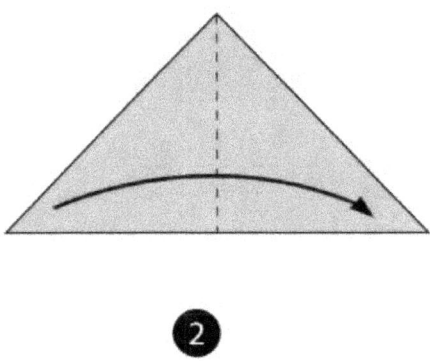

Fold the left triangle corner over to meet the right corner (in half from left to right). Crease well, and then unfold this so it is back to a triangle.

Step 3

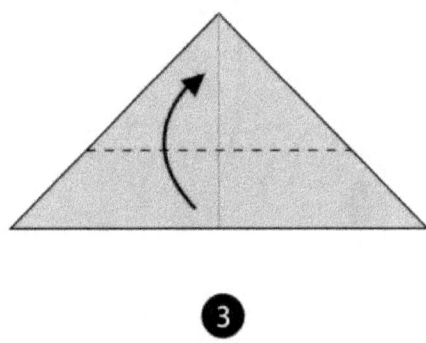

Fold the bottom half of the triangle up, leaving a bit of the top point of the triangle peeking out (take a peek at the picture to see what I mean). Crease well.

Step 4

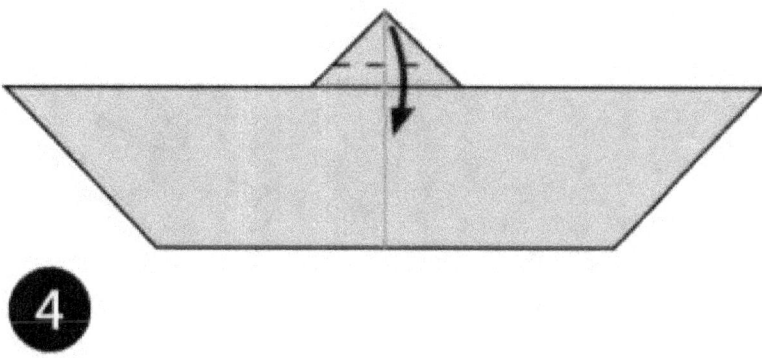

Fold down the top point you left peeking out in half from the top to bottom so that it overlaps the other piece you just folded (see the picture below). This is going to be your bat's cute little face!

Step 5

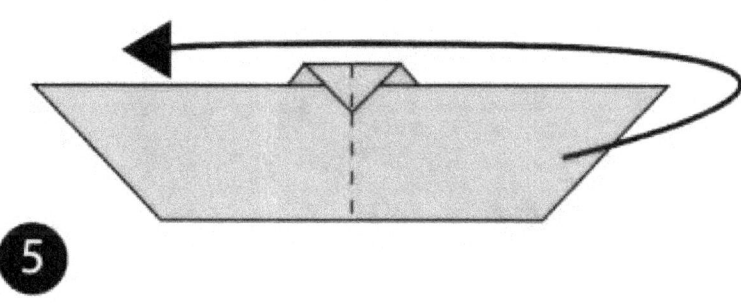

Fold in half from the right remaining corner back to the left. Crease well.

Step 6

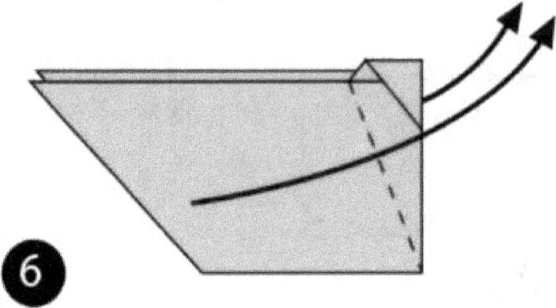

Fold the top wing over and up a bit (follow the dotted line). Repeat this on the other side to the other wing.

Step 7

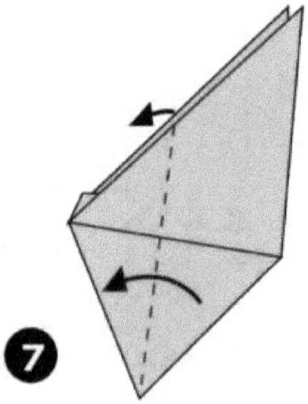

Fold in half, taking the right side over to the left (again, follow the dotted line in the picture)

Step 8

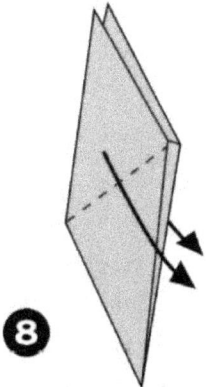

Fold down the top point in half. Repeat this fold for the top point on the other side.

Step 9

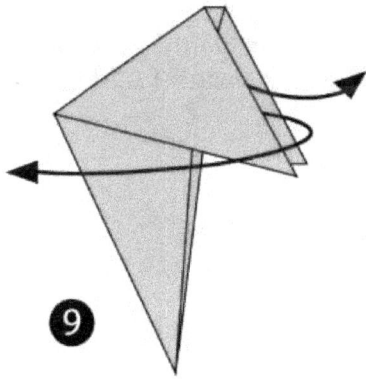

See the arrows in the picture? Pull each side as shown in each direction of the arrows.

Step 10

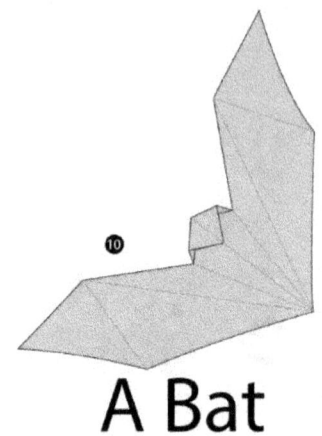

A Bat

Flatten things out, and take a look! You're done! You can decorate your bat, draw on a face and other details, or leave it as is.

Fun fact: There are over 1000 different varieties of bats. Which does your origami bat look like most?

Did you know... before "origami", the practice of paper folding was called "orikata" which means "folded shape".

Chapter 12: Bear Cub

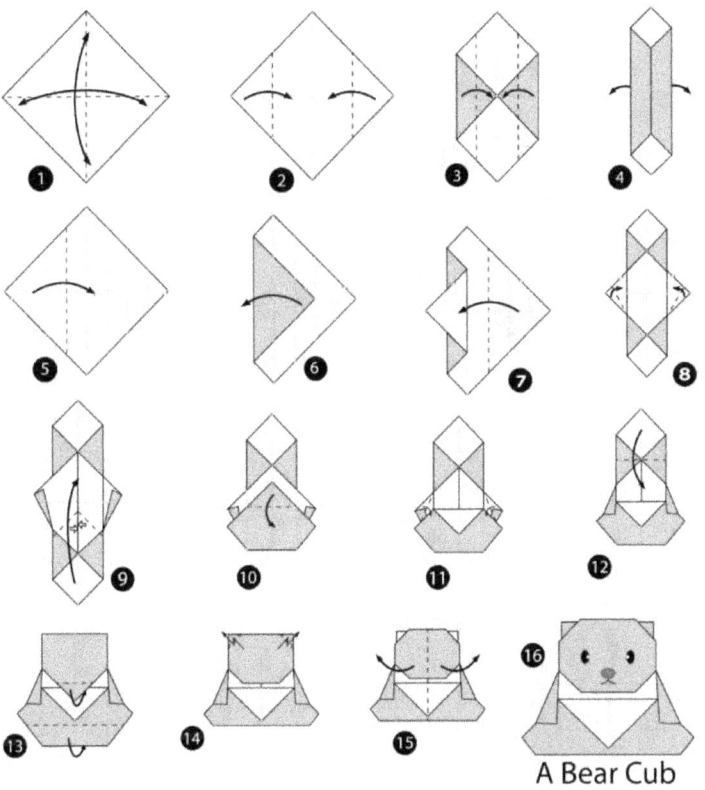

A Bear Cub

Start with your paper flat on your surface, color (or pattern) side face down, in the shape of a diamond. The colored side will be the outside of your cute little bear cub.

Step 1

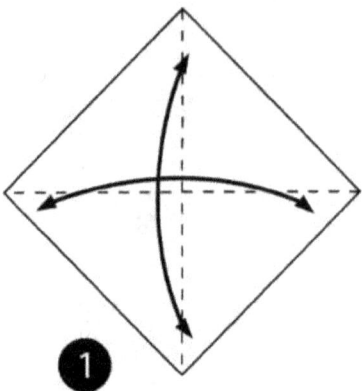

Fold in half from the left corner to the right, unfold. Now fold in half from top to bottom, and unfold. You'll have another cross in the center like many of our other projects.

Step 2

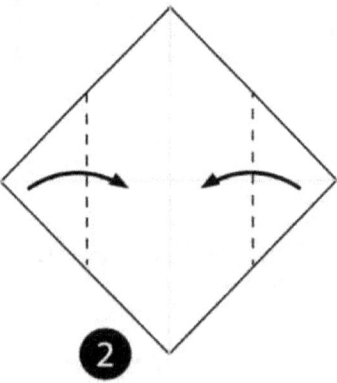

Fold the left and right corners to meet in the middle on the center crease, as shown in the picture.

Step 3

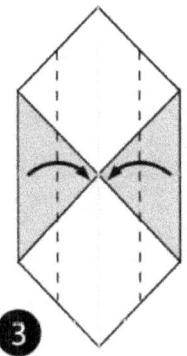

Fold the left edge to the center crease, and repeat for the right edge.

Step 4

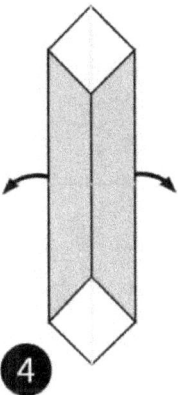

Unfold all of the folds you've made so far. I know it seems odd, but trust me!

Step 5

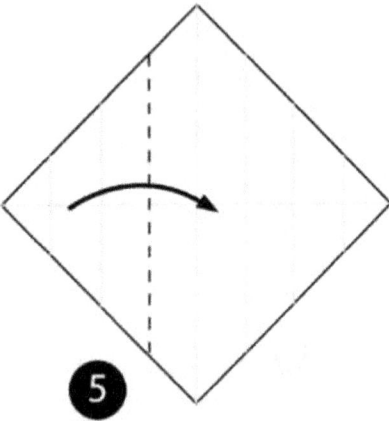

See all of the creases you've made? There are eight all together. Now, fold the left corner along the dotted line as shown, so that the point rests on the sixth crease counting from the left.

Step 6

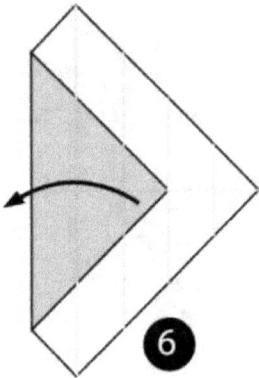

Fold the top flap to the left along the very middle crease as shown in the picture.

Step 7

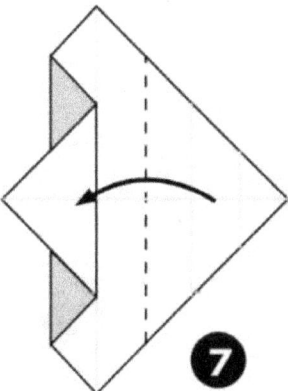

Repeat steps 5, 6, and 7 on the right side to match the left.

Step 8

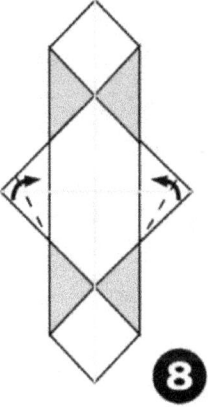

See the dotted lines? Fold each corner along the dotted lines shown.

Step 9

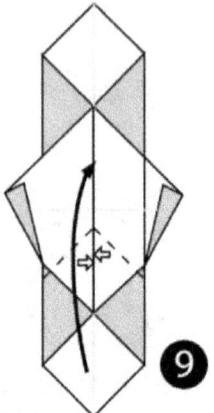

See the white arrows? Yes, it's another squash fold! You're getting good at this by now! Open up the pockets slightly where the white arrows are located and as you fold over the very bottom corner upwards, the pockets should open up at the same time and then flatten them as you complete the fold. See picture below for confirmation.

Step 10

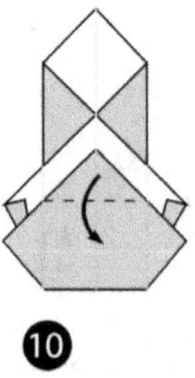

Follow the arrow, folding down along the dotted line.

Step 11

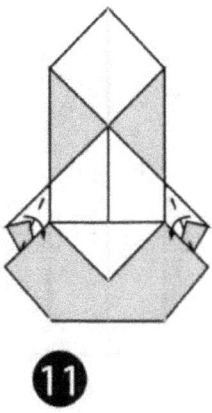

Lift the left side open a bit and fold inward and over, as shown in the picture. Repeat on the right side. These will make the bears little arms.

Step 12

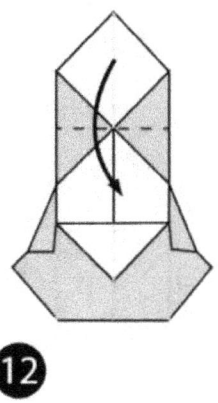

Fold the top point down along the dotted line. See picture below for confirmation.

Step 13

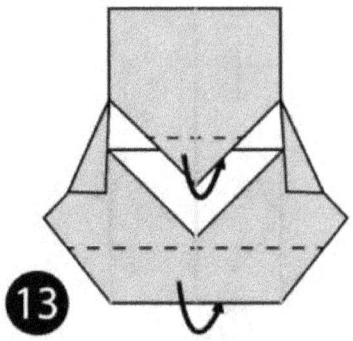

See the dotted line at the top? Fold backwards along the dotted line, tucking under. Fold backwards along the lower dotted line as well.

Step 14

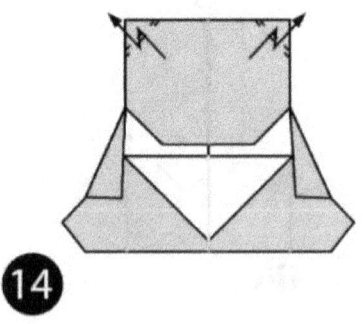

Lift the left edge up a bit and fold inward along the dotted line but still leaving out the tip. This is sometimes called a step fold because it forms a "step" like a staircase; check the "folds" chapter if you need to. Repeat this on the right side.

Step 15

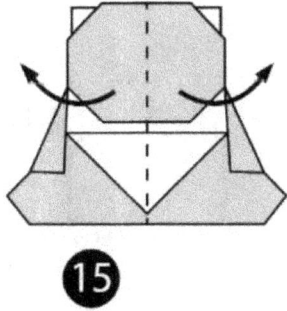

Fold the entire piece in half making a crease in the middle, then unfold it again.

Step 16

A Bear Cub

Draw on your bear cub's face, and you're ready to tame! Give your bear a pretty necklace or a bow tie (maybe this cub is fancy!) and let him join your other animal friends.

Fun Fact: Bears have an extremely good sense of smell, better than dogs, and maybe even better than any other animal!

Did you know… the origami crane has become an international symbol for peace. An organization called "Wings for Peace" made the world's largest paper crane in 1999. It was 1,750 pounds and 215 feet tall.

Chapter 13: Lion

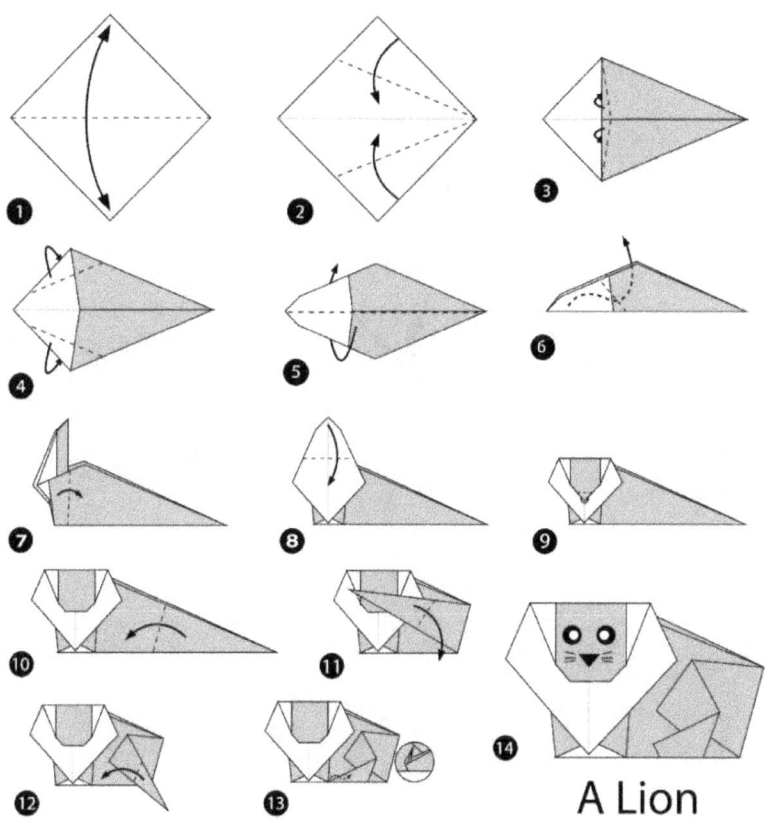

Real tigers and lions don't really get along, but this paper lion can be your paper tiger's best friend! Start with your paper flat on your work surface in the shape of a diamond, with the color (or pattern) side down. This color will soon be the "fur" color of your lion.

Step 1

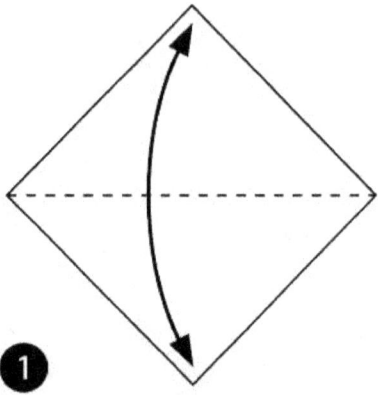

Fold the top corner down to the bottom, as shown in the picture, then unfold again.

Step 2

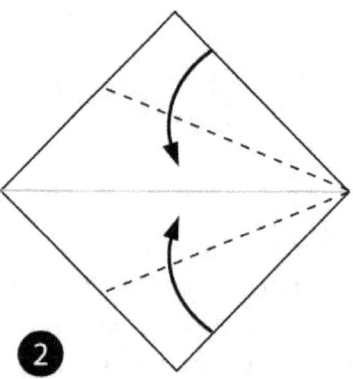

See the dotted lines? Fold along them so that the edges meet at the center crease.

Step 3

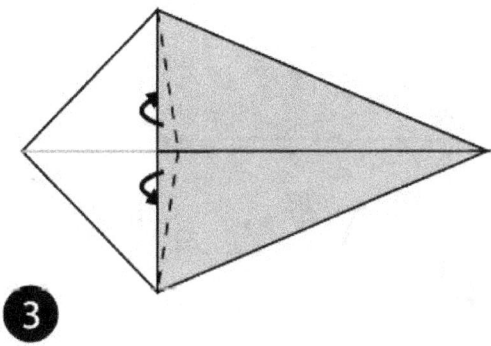

Fold along the dotted lines, but folding backwards tucking in.

Step 4

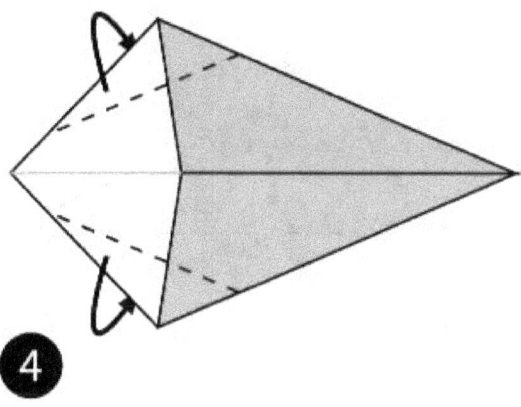

See the dotted lines? Fold backwards along them.

Step 5

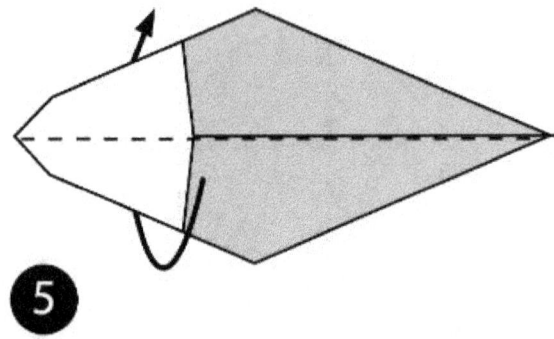

Fold in half as shown, by folding the bottom half under.

Step 6

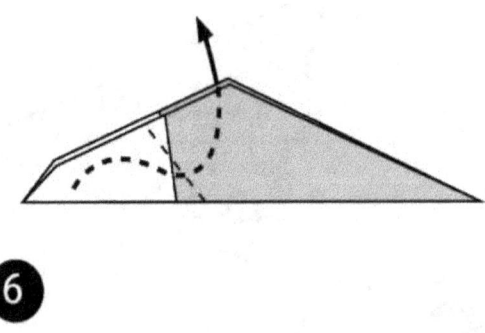

Fold upward and inward, pushing in, as shown in the picture (this is the squash fold again).

Step 7

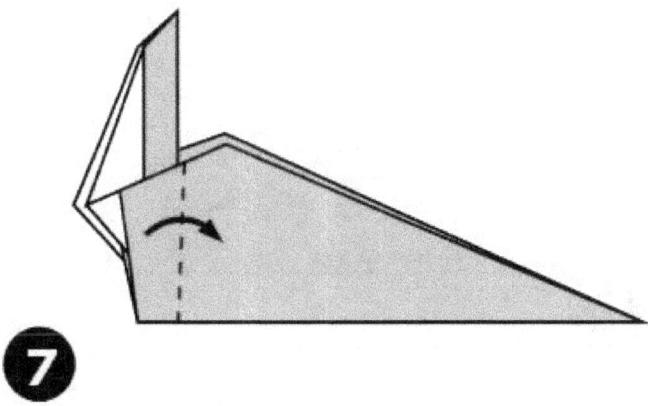

Fold the top flap along the dotted line as shown.

Step 8

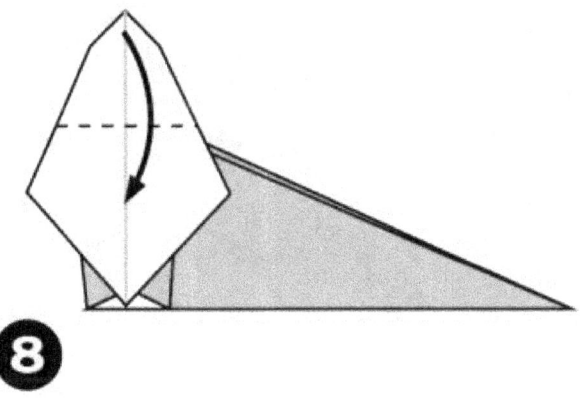

Fold down on the dotted line like you see in the picture.

Step 9

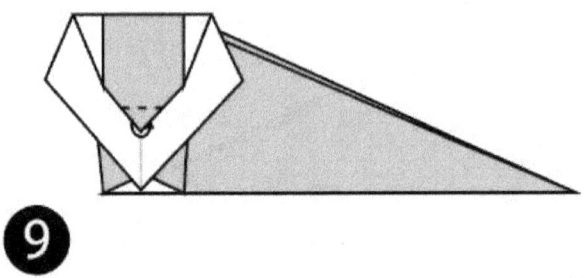

See the dotted line? Fold the little point backwards, tucking in as shown in the picture.

Step 10

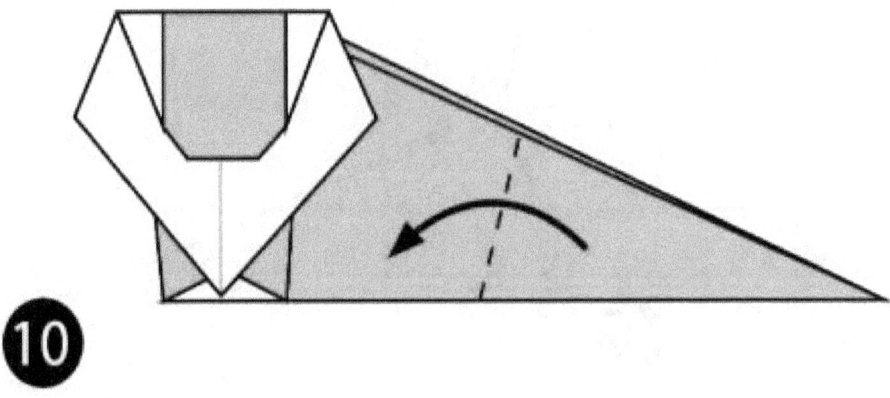

Following the dotted line, fold the point over from the right towards the left.

Step 11

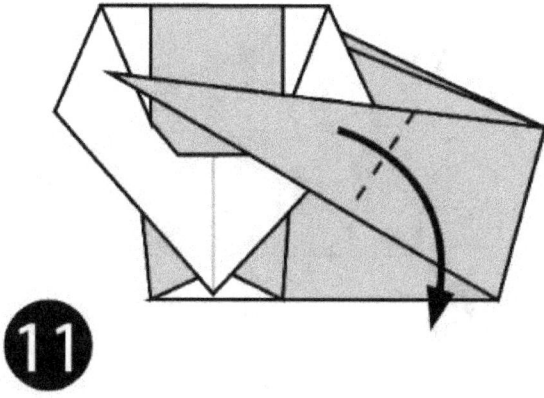

Follow the dotted line again, folding the point down and back towards the right.

Step 12

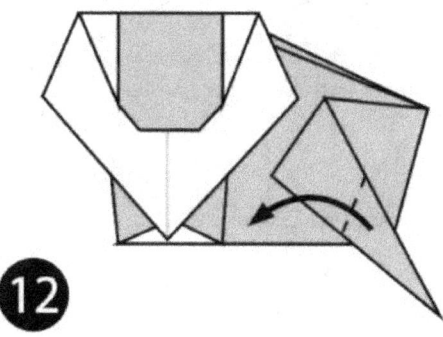

One more time, fold the tip back up and to the left so that it lines up along the bottom edge.

Step 13

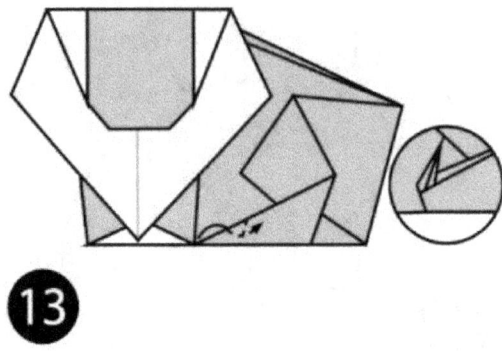

Fold the very tip inward, tucking it in.

Step 14

A Lion

Congratulations! Draw on your lion's face, decorate his mane, and give him a name!

Fun Fact: Both male and female lions can roar. Their roar can be heard up to five miles away!

Did you know... origami has become such a popular form of art that there are now several origami associations that have been formed all over the world. There is the Origami Center of America and the British Origami Society, among others. Most major cities now have "origami masters".

Chapter 14: Penguin

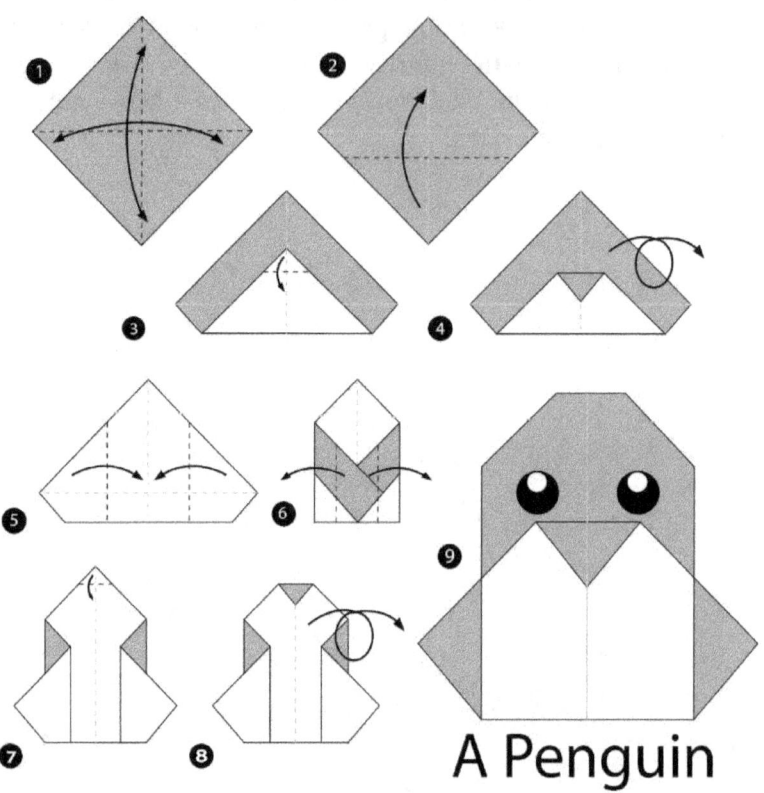

A Penguin

Were penguins one of the animals you guessed that live in Antarctica? This paper one doesn't have to live in cold weather, though. Maybe this penguin is a tropical penguin! Start with your paper flat on your work surface with the color (or pattern) side facing up. Lay your paper out so that it is in the shape of a diamond.

Step 1

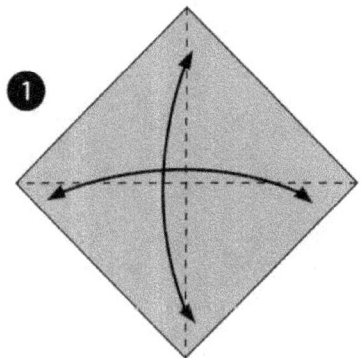

Fold the left corner over to the right, folding in half, then unfold it again. Repeat this with the bottom corned folded up to the top. Unfold once again.

Step 2

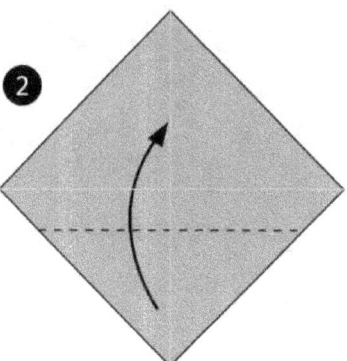

Following the dotted line, fold the lower corner up, creasing where you see the dotted line in the picture.

Step 3

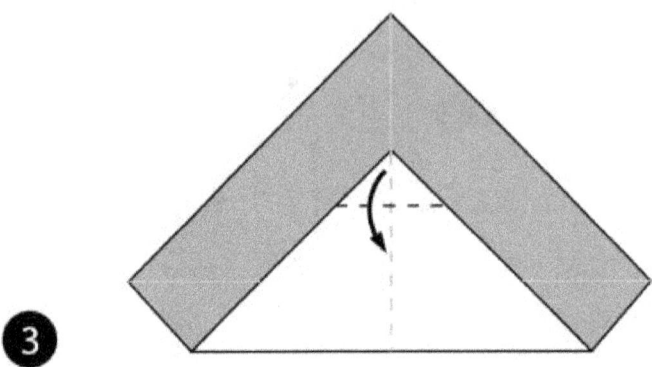

Following the dotted line, fold the top point down as shown.

Step 4

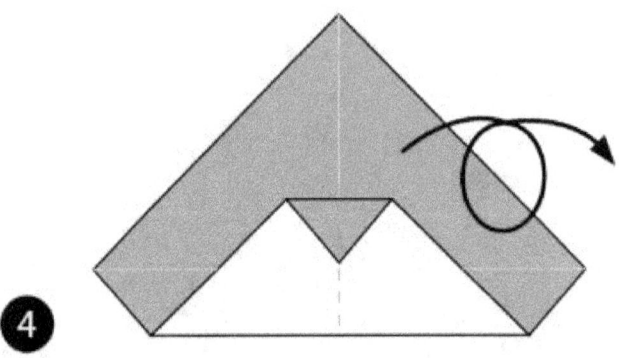

Turn the whole piece over.

Step 5

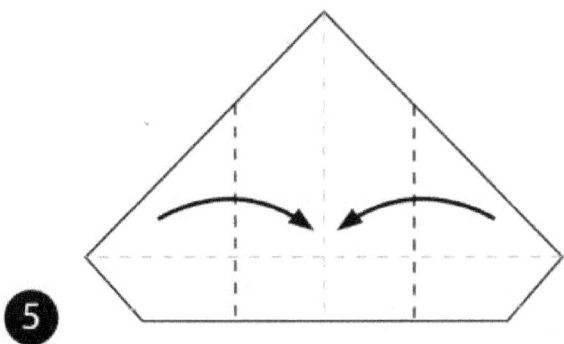

Fold the left corner a bit past the center line, as shown. Then fold the right in the same way. The two will overlap a little in the middle.

Step 6

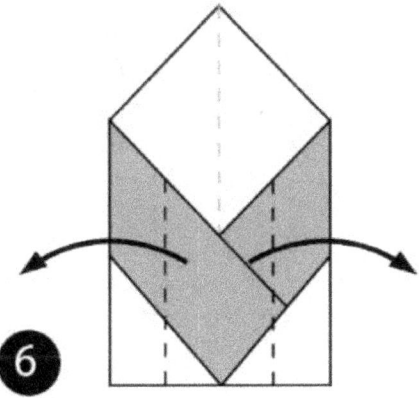

Follow the arrows and fold along the dotted lines, doing the left side first, then the right.

Step 7

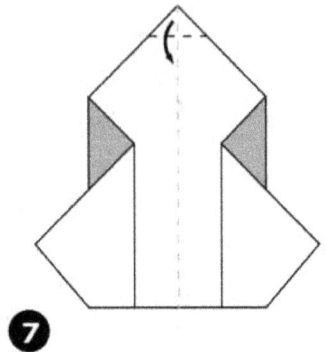

Fold the top point down, as shown.

Step 8

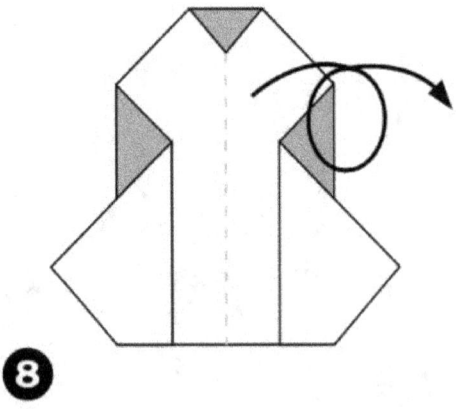

Turn the whole piece over.

Step 9

A Penguin

Woo! You're done! Draw on eyes, color the beak, and maybe give your penguin a scarf to keep him warm. Unless your penguin really is tropical, then maybe give him a swim suit and a cold drink!

Fun Fact: There are many varieties of penguins. For example, Emperor Penguins are the tallest species, standing about 4 feet tall. The smallest is the Little Blue Penguin, which is only roughly 16 inches. The fastest penguin species is the Gentoo Penguin, which can swim up to 22 miles per hour.

Did you know... Akira Yoshizawa is often considered the Grand Master of origami. He created over 50,000 origami models. He also invented a method called wet-folding and developed a method of drawing origami instructions.

Chapter 15: Platypus

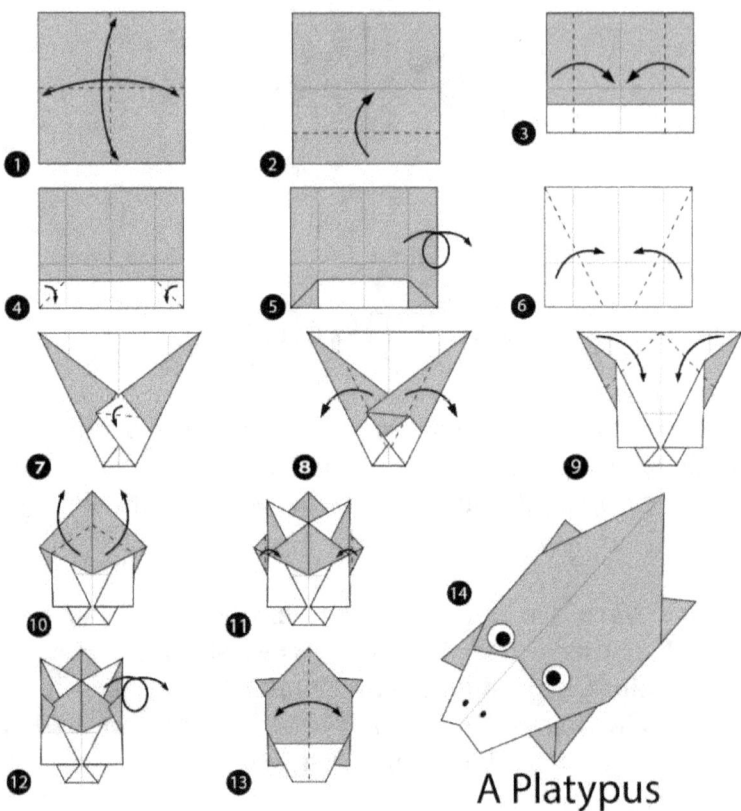

A Platypus

Have you ever heard of a platypus? It's a very unique creature! For this animal, instead of putting your paper color side down, place it flat on your work surface in the shape of a square with the color side facing up.

Step 1

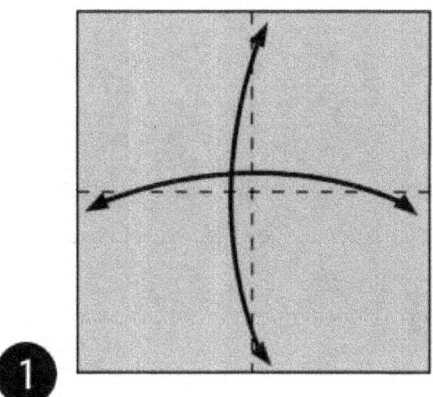

Fold the top edge to the bottom edge, and unfold it again. Repeat this with the left edge to the right edge, and unfold again.

Step 2

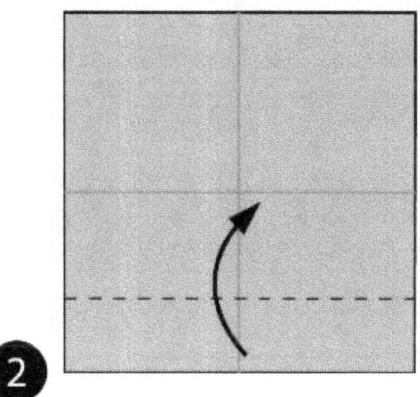

Following the dotted line, fold upward almost to the center crease, but not quite.

Step 3

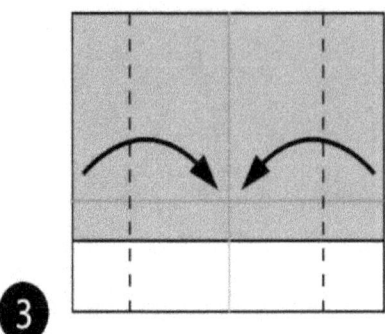

Fold both the left edge, and then the right edge, in to the center crease so that they meet, then unfold again.

Step 4

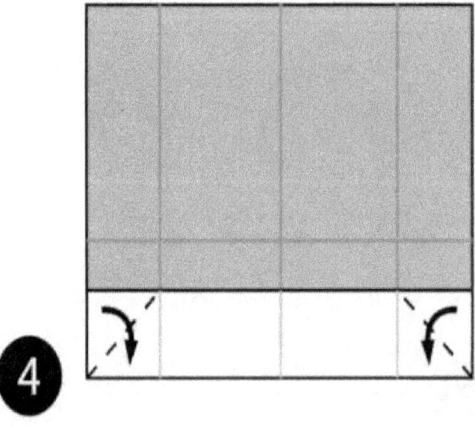

Following the dotted lines, fold both the left and right corners down to the bottom edge as shown.

Step 5

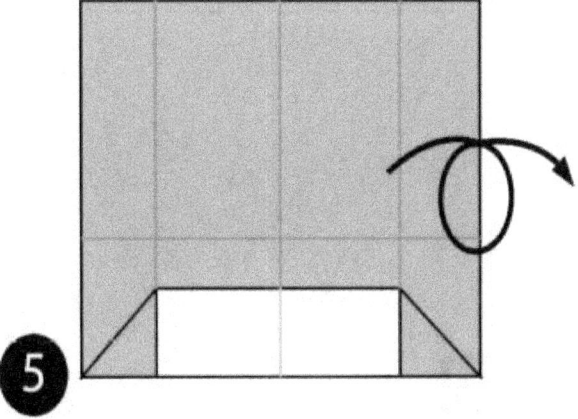

Turn the whole piece over.

Step 6

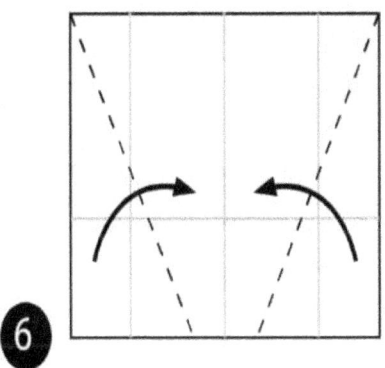

Following the dotted lines, fold the left side over, and then the right side. The right side will overlap the left, as shown on the next step.

Step 7

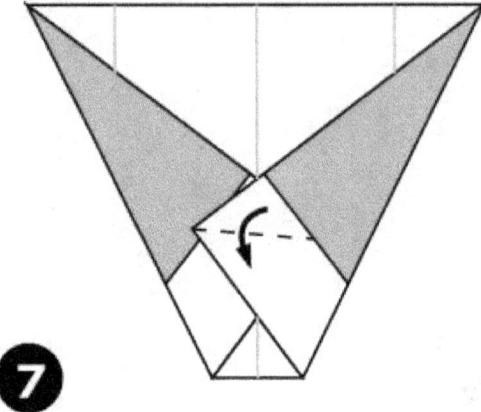

See the dotted line and the arrow? Following the arrow, fold down the corner along the dotted line.

Step 8

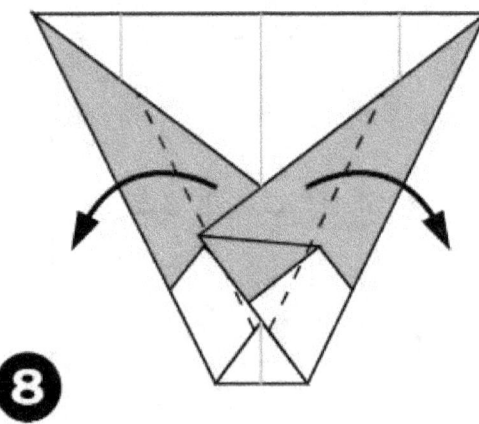

Follow the dotted lines and fold the right side first (the part on top) and then the left.

Step 9

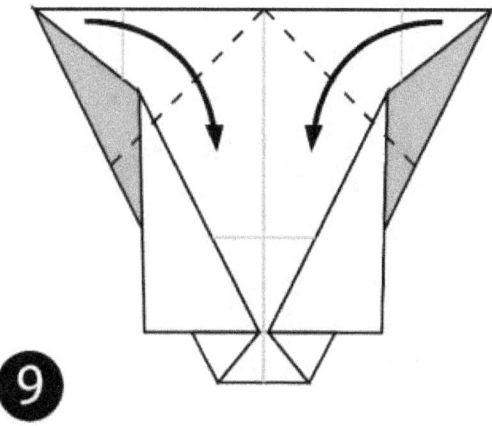

Fold the top two corners down in order to meet the center crease, as shown.

Step 10

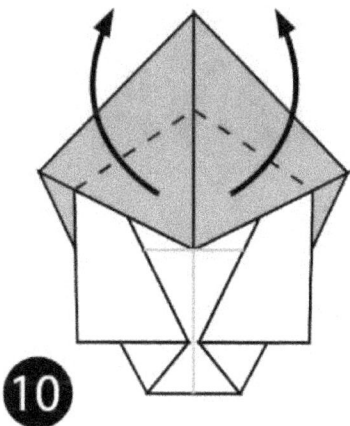

Following the dotted lines, fold up and outward a bit for both sides, as shown.

Step 11

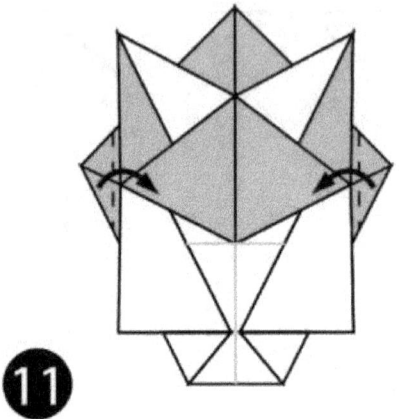

Fold the left and right "tabs" over as shown.

Step 12

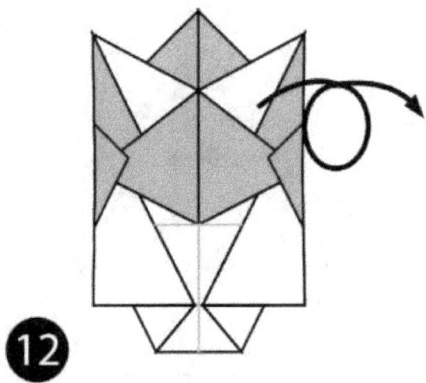

Turn the whole piece over.

Step 13

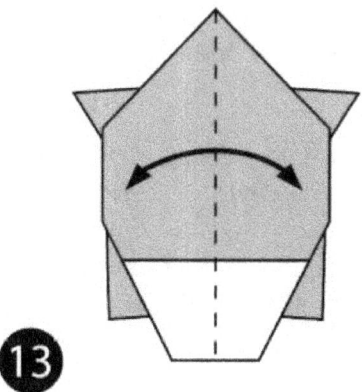

Fold in half with a mountain fold as shown and crease, then unfold.

Step 14

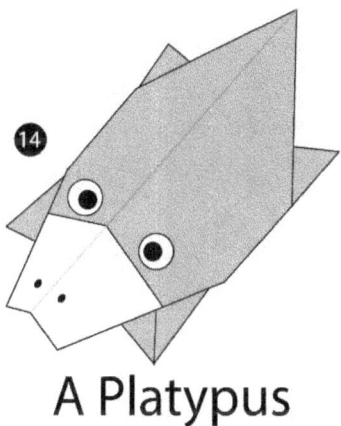

A Platypus

Draw eyes and other details to spruce up your new friend! Maybe give him some cool sunglasses?

Fun Fact: When the platypus was first brought from Australia to Britain, people didn't believe that it was a real animal because of its strange appearance. It has a paddle-like tail like a beaver, a furry body much like an otter, and webbed feet and a bill like a duck.

Did you know… the world record for longest origami snake is **152.52625 feet long. This world record was made on March 11th 2001 in Singapore. There is also a record for the longest caterpillar, which is 2,128 feet. It was made in Germany in October of 2004 by 60 men with 25,000 sheets of paper.**

Chapter 16: Gorilla

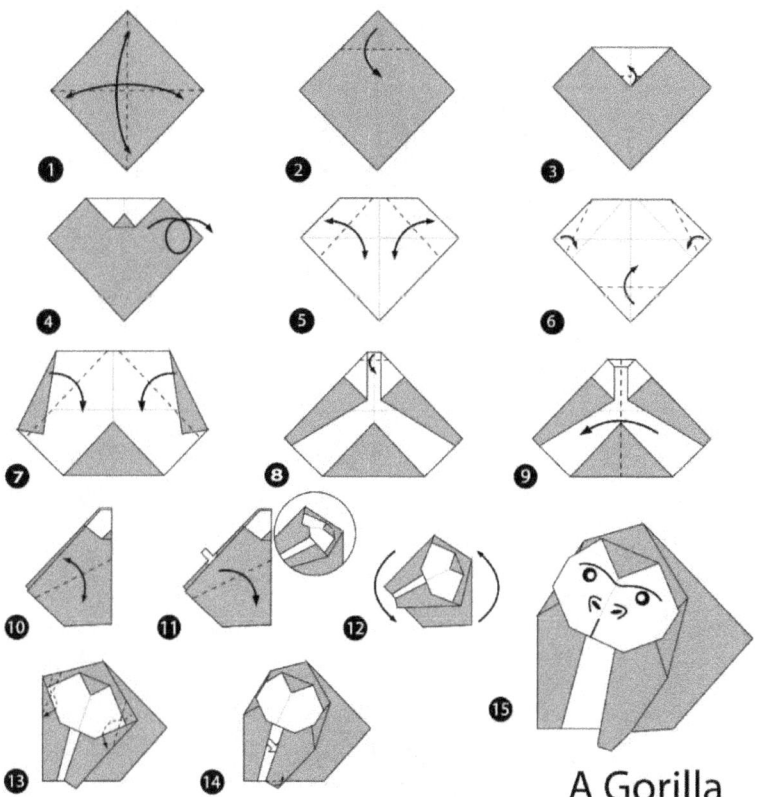

A Gorilla

We've got felines, canines, fish, bears, birds… now we need a primate! Start this project with the paper flat on your work surface, color (or pattern) side facing up again this time, placed down in the shape of a diamond.

Step 1

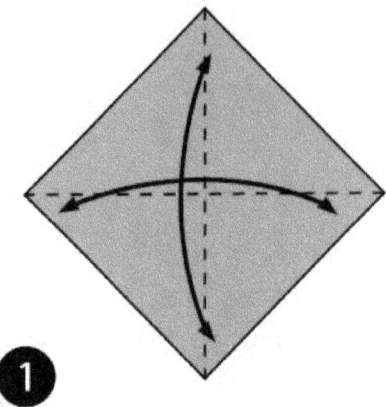

Fold the left corner over to the right, crease well and then unfold again. Next, fold the top corner down to the bottom, crease, and unfold as well.

Step 2

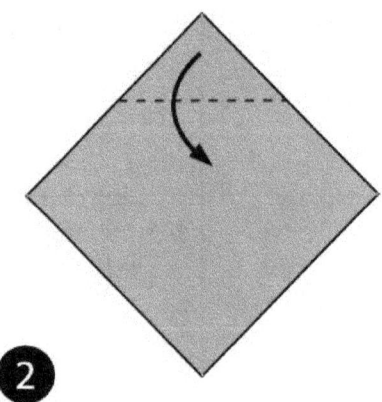

Fold the top point down to the center as shown in the picture.

Step 3

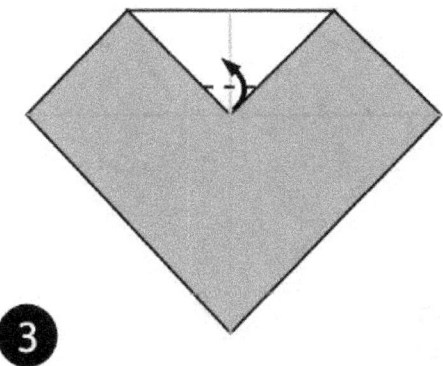

See the little dotted line and arrow? Fold the little point up, as shown.

Step 4

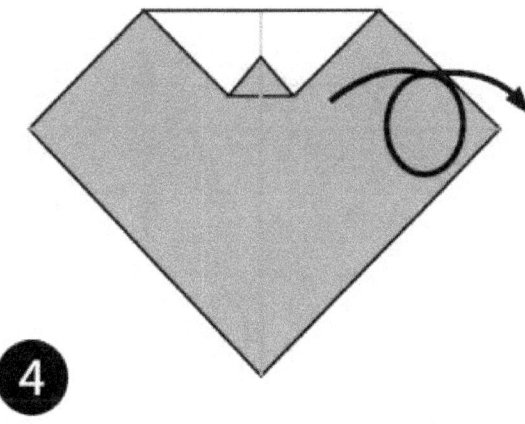

You probably remember what this symbol means, and it's super easy! Just turn the whole piece over.

Step 5

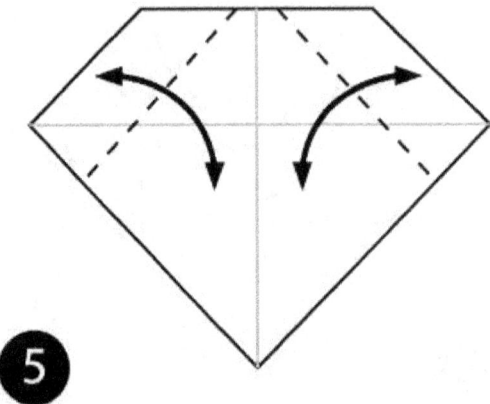

Take a look at the dotted lines and arrows on both sides. Fold along the dotted lines in the direction of the arrows as show. Remember to crease well, then unfold.

Step 6

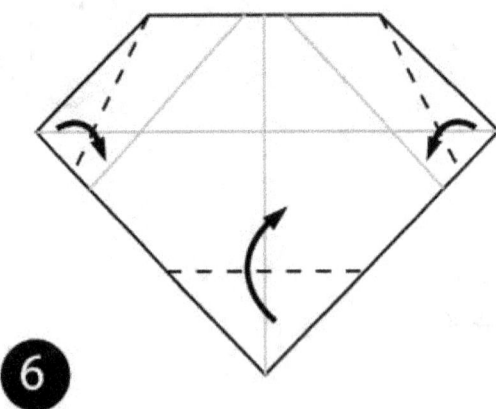

Here you have 3 folds to make, but don't worry, it's pretty easy. Fold the left corner over so that the tip of it goes just a little past the crease you made on the left in step 5. Now do the same thing with the right side. Finally, fold the bottom corner up as shown in the picture by the dotted line.

Step 7

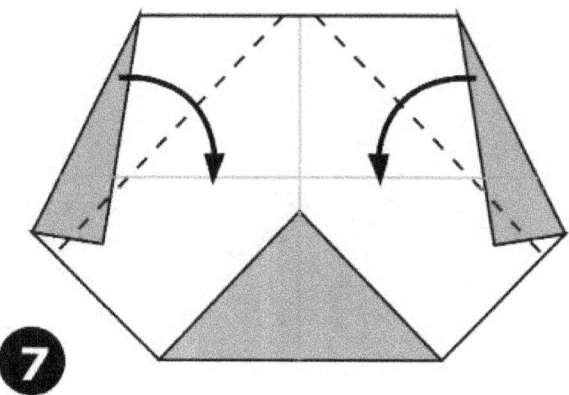

Fold along the dotted line on the left in the direction of the arrow as shown. Do the same thing following the dotted line on the right side.

Step 8

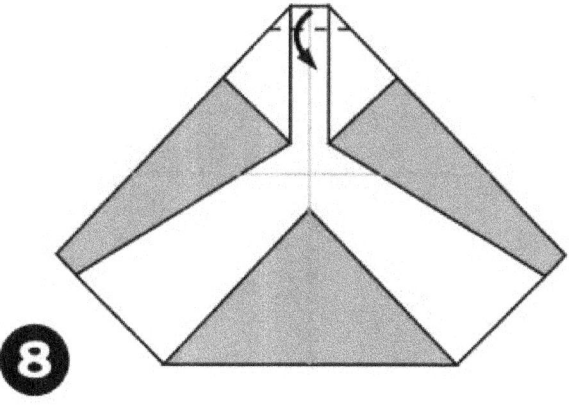

See the little dotted line at the top again? Fold down along the dotted line as shown in the picture.

Step 9

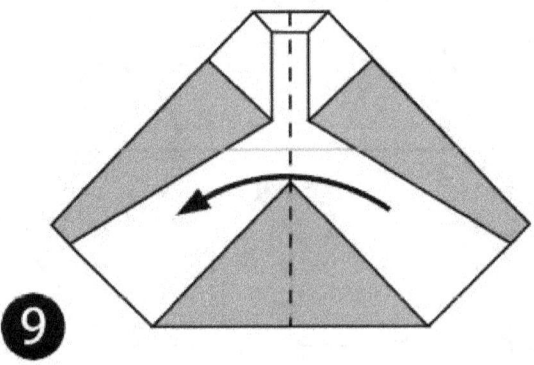

Fold the right half over to the left, so that the project is folded in half.

Step 10

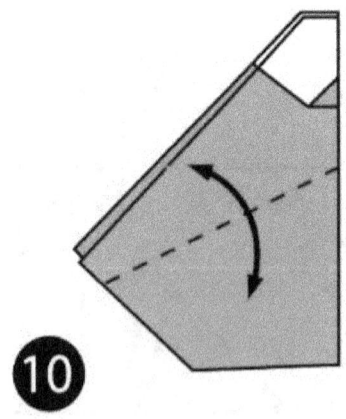

Fold along the dotted line downwards as shown in the picture. Crease well, and then unfold. Repeat these steps again but folding along the dotted lines backwards.

Step 11

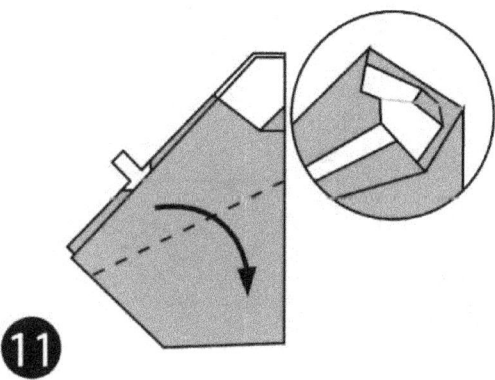

See where the white arrow is? Lift this up a bit so it starts to open and then do a squash fold along the dotted line as shown. You can see what it should look like in step 12.

Step 12

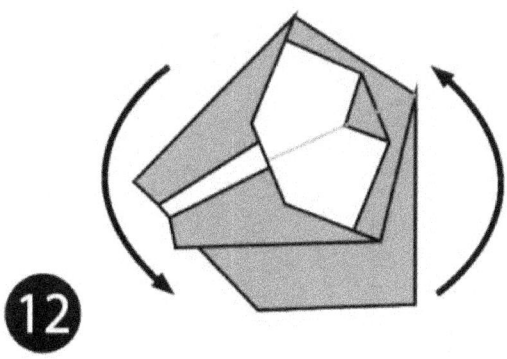

Rotate your origami project to the left, as shown by the arrows. You can see what I mean and how it should look in step 13.

Step 13

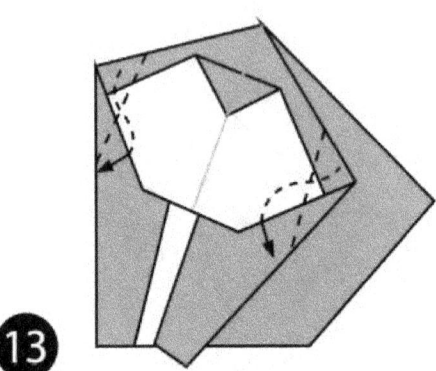

See the arrows and dotted lines on both sides? Do a pocket fold, tucking the points inside. Remember to do this on both sides, as shown in the picture. You're almost done!

Step 14

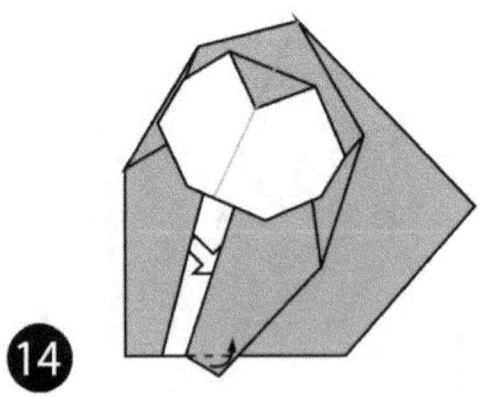

See the white arrow and dotted line? Lift up the side that the white arrow points to, and do a pocket fold where the dotted line is shown, tucking inside.

Step 15

A Gorilla

Boom! Your gorilla just needs some eyes, nose, and other details you might want to add, and then he (or she) is done!

Fun Fact: After chimpanzees and bonobos, gorillas are the closest living relatives to humans. They share about 95% of their DNA with people, and our two species come from the same common ancestor.

Did you know... Alongside the largest origami projects, there are also world records for the smallest pieces. Professor Watanabe in Japan folded the smallest paper crane; it's just 1mm in size and was made by using tweezers and a microscope. A Frenchmen named Eric Roudiere made the smallest origami chicken at just 1.5 mm x 1.5 mm x 1.19 mm. March 16th 1995, a kid named Christian Thorp Frederiksen who was just 12 years of age made the smallest paper aircraft, which is 2.5 mm x 1 mm, and a man

named Christian Elbrandt folded a 2.7 mm origami frog that can jump to 103mm.

Chapter 17: Swan

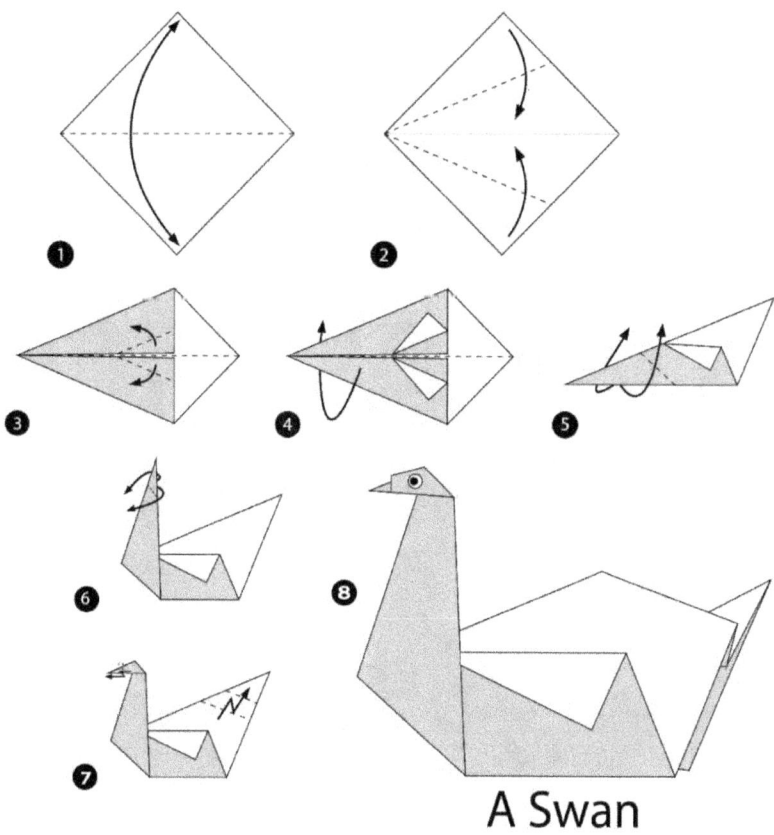

A Swan

We have a penguin (they swim in the water), so maybe it needs another feathered water friend. Start with your paper flat on your work surface, color (or pattern) side down, in the shape of a diamond. This color facing down will be the outside, or "feathers", of your swan.

Step 1

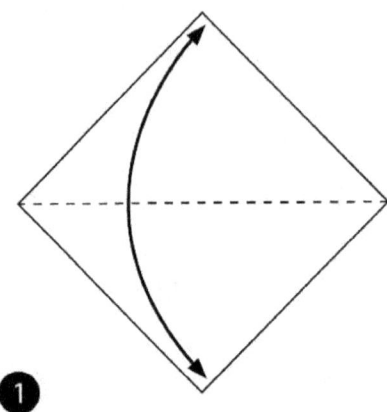

Fold the bottom point up to meet the top point, making a center crease. Unfold again.

Step 2

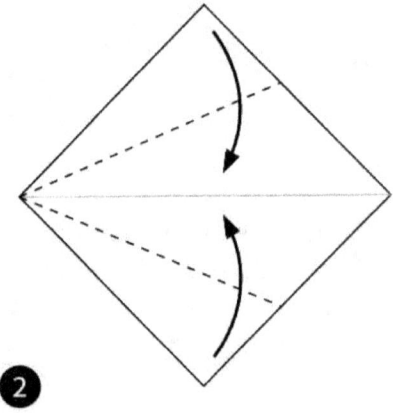

See the dotted lines? Fold each edge along the dotted lines meeting the middle crease as shown.

Step 3

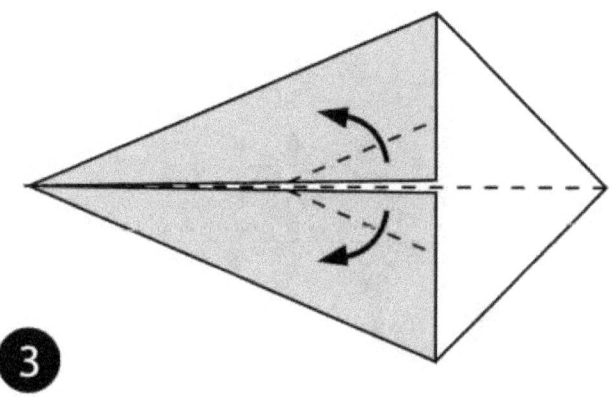

Fold the inner corners out along the dotted lines.

Step 4

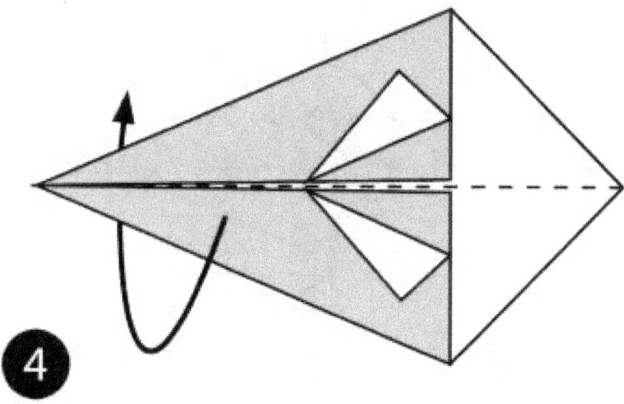

Fold the whole piece in half with a mountain fold by folding the two sides together.

Step 5

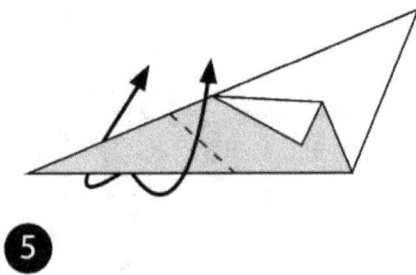

See the arrows? Lift the point upward, following the arrows, and fold in the center, tucking, with a pocket fold.

Step 6

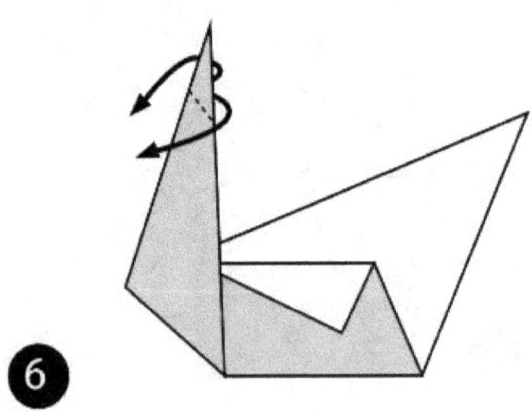

Repeat the technique you used in step five on the very tip here, as shown.

Step 7

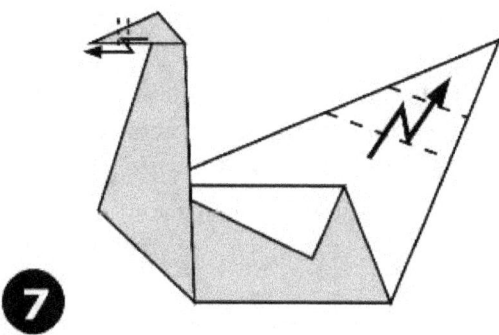

See the dotted lines at the tail? Fold down and inward along the dotted lines, doing a stair fold. Crease well. Fold the beak inwards slightly using a stair fold.

Step 8

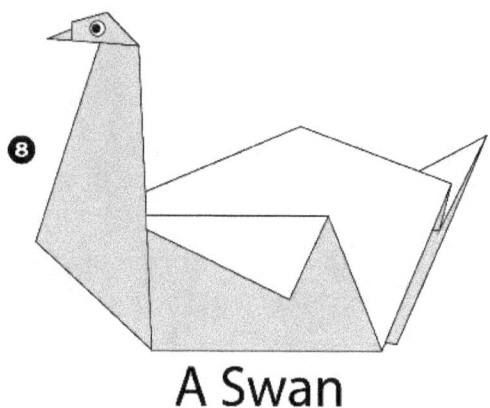

A Swan

Now you have an elegant swan! Just like the story of the ugly duckling transforming into a beautiful swan, you have transformed a regular sheet of paper into a special paper swan.

Fun Fact: Swans are the largest member of the duck and goose family. They have over 25,000 feathers. A male swan is called a cob, while a female swan is called a pen.

Did you know... In Mexico, candy wrappers are often weaved into handbags, jewelry, purses, and other accessories. This helps the environment by reusing paper that would normally be trash. It also helps the Mexican economy.

Chapter 18: Giraffe

Our parade of animals continues with this cute giraffe. Like many of our other animal origami projects, start this one by placing your paper on a flat work surface with the color (or pattern) side down, and so that it is in the shape of a diamond.

Step 1

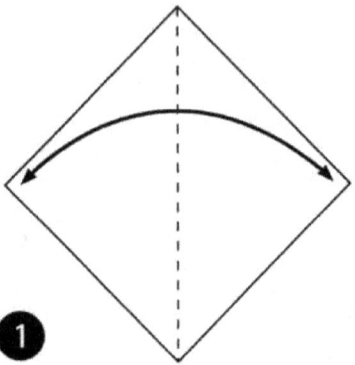

Fold the paper in half from left to right, crease well, and then unfold it again.

Step 2

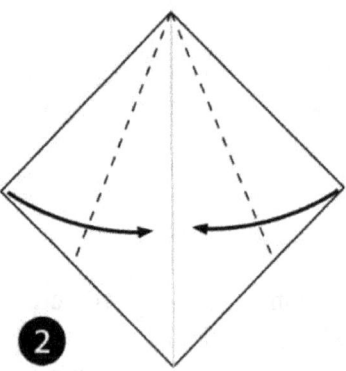

Following the dotted lines, fold the two outer corners in to meet at the center crease.

Step 3

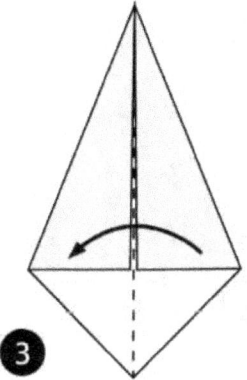

Now fold in half along the center line, as shown in the picture.

Step 4

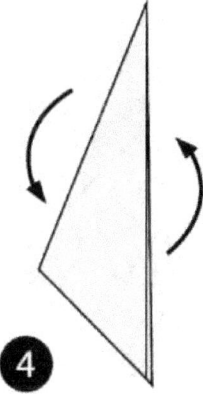

Turn the whole piece to the left, as shown, so that the top point is pointed up and to the left (like the picture).

Step 5

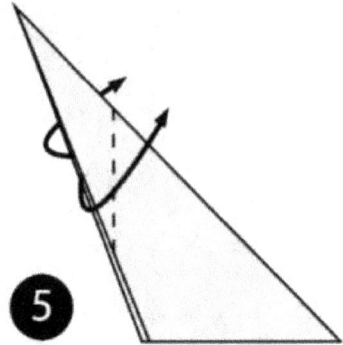

Following the arrows, fold the piece back and out, starting a hood fold.

Step 6

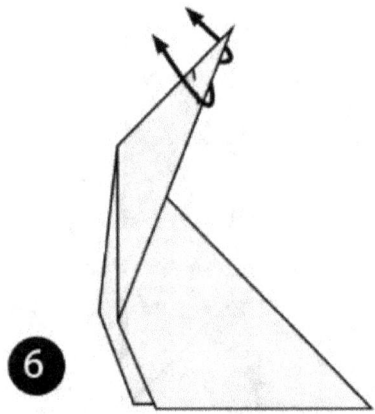

Complete the hood fold from above, creasing well.

Step 7

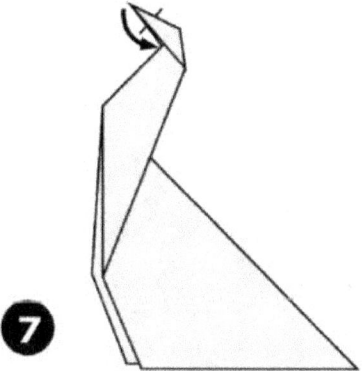

Now do a regular pocket fold on the very tip, folding inwards as shown.

Step 8

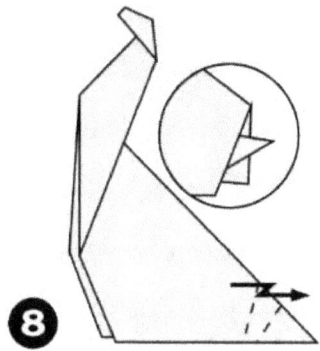

Perform a stair fold at the tail as shown in the image above.

Step 9

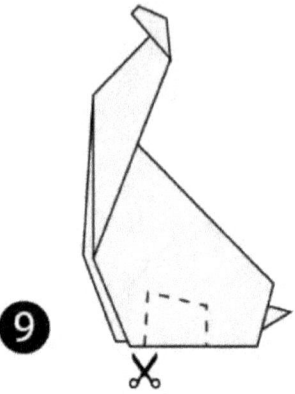

Ask an adult for some help with this part if you need to because it uses scissors. Cut along the dotted lines shown here, and remove the piece you cut out.

Step 10

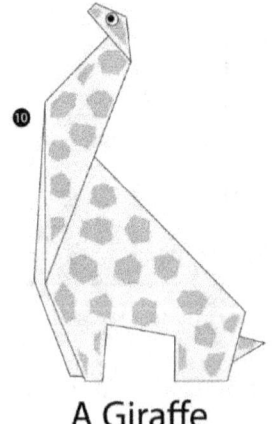

A Giraffe

Add eyes, and spots (or stripes, or stars, or whatever you want!), and your giraffe is all ready to play with the other animals.

Fun Fact: Giraffes are the tallest mammals on Earth. Their legs alone are taller than most people at about 6 feet tall. Even with their very long necks, their long legs actually make their neck and head unable to reach the ground when they bend forward.

Did you know... origami isn't just fun, it is also used for educational purposes. Folding origami can help better your understanding of geometry, visualization skills, learning fractions in math, and problem solving, just to name a few!

Chapter 19: Squirrel

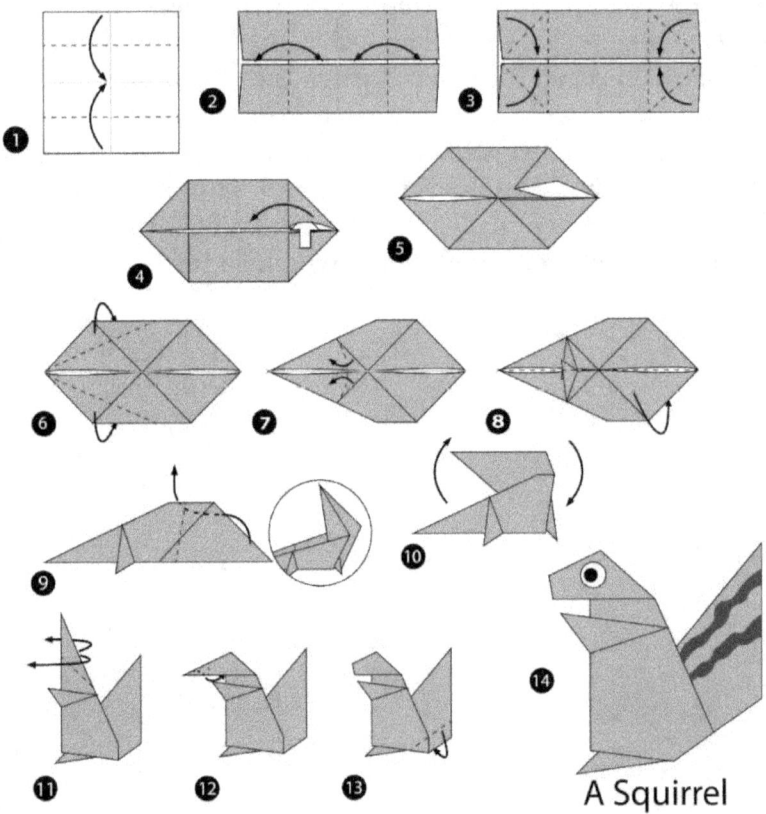

A Squirrel

For our last animal buddy, we have a little squirrel. Start with your paper flat on your work surface, color (or pattern) side down, in the shape of a square. Prepare your paper by folding in half from top to bottom, and from left to right, and unfold. Use these creases as a guide.

Step 1

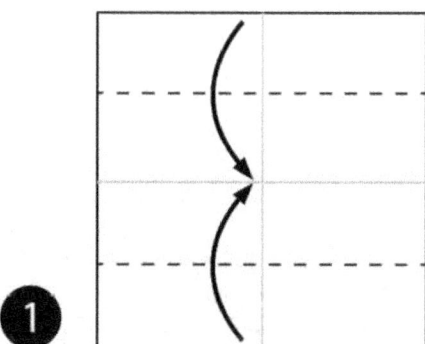

Fold the top edge down to the center crease. Fold the bottom edge up to the center crease, meeting with the top edge in the middle. Crease well.

Step 2

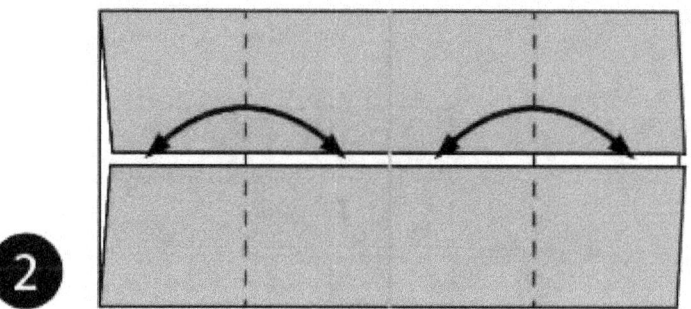

Fold the left edge in order to meet the center crease. Then fold the right in to the center crease as well, meeting with the left edge. Crease well, and unfold again.

Step 3

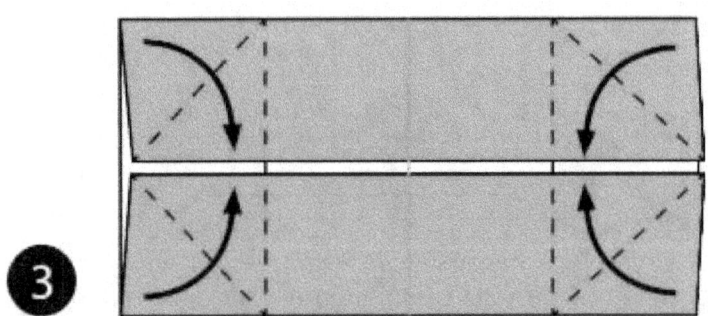

Fold the top left corner down to the center line as shown in the picture. Do the same thing on the other three remaining corners.

Step 4

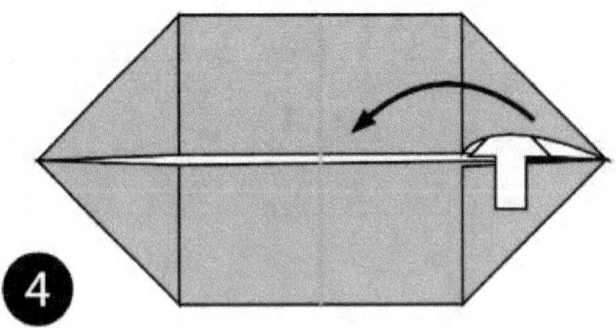

You should now have a pocket where the white arrow is. Lift it open and flatten it with a squash fold.

Step 5

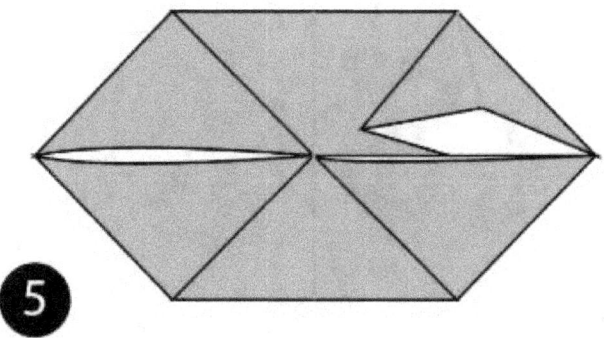

Repeat step four on the three remaining pockets, as shown.

Step 6

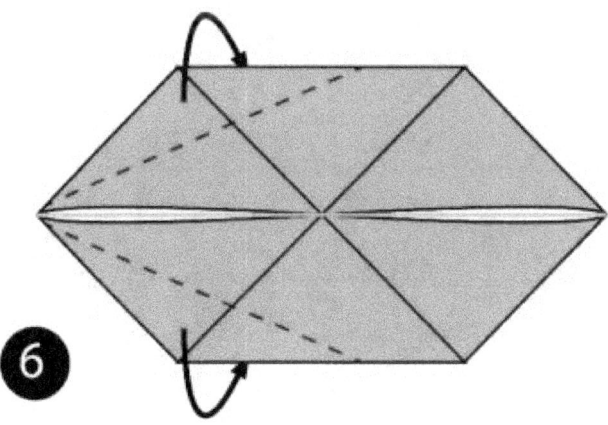

Following the dotted lines, fold these two sections backwards with a mountain fold.

Step 7

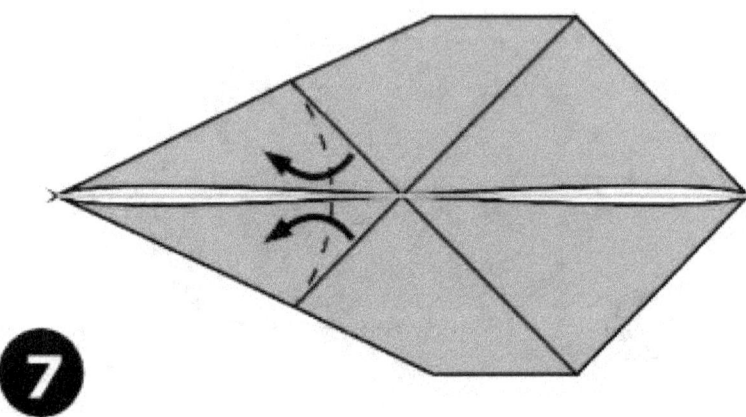

See the dotted lines and arrows? Fold inward along the dotted lines, so that these areas are being tucked in.

Step 8

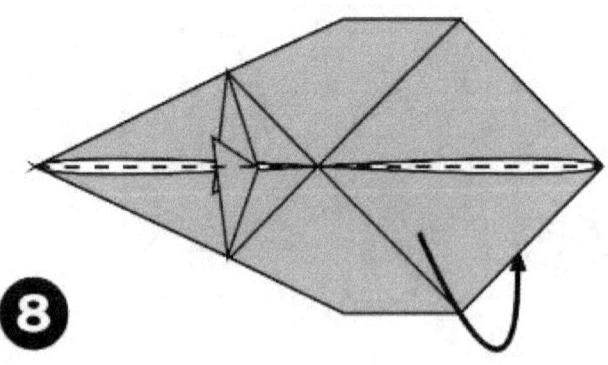

Fold in half by tucking the bottom part behind with a mountain fold, as shown by the arrow.

Step 9

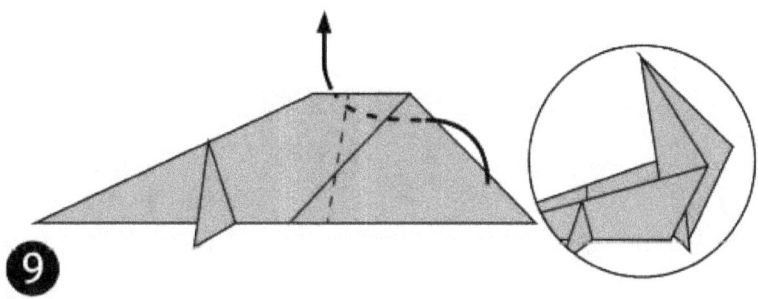

Follow the dotted lines, and fold inward, tucking in, using a pocket fold.

Step 10

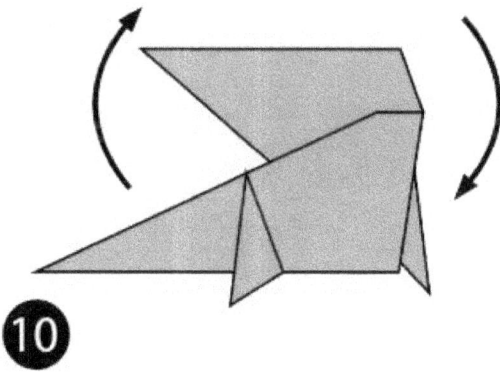

Rotate the piece a bit to the right, so that the points on the left are now at the top.

Step 11

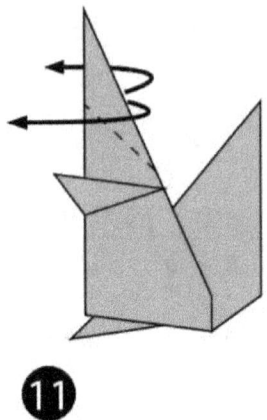

This part is tricky, but you can do it! Fold along the dotted line, going inward and tucking, and then flattening out. This is the hood fold again.

Step 12

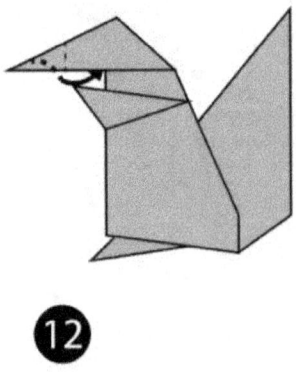

Now use an inward fold where the dotted line is, tucking the point inside.

Step 13

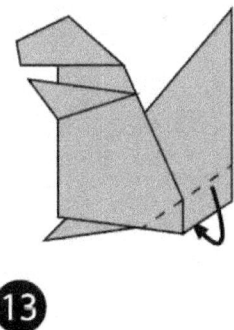

See the dotted line? Fold along the dotted line, folding the edge up inside.

Step 14

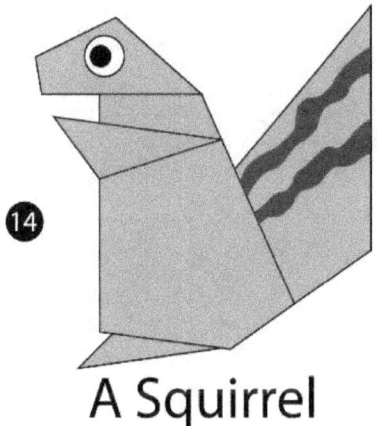

A Squirrel

Fantastic! Add an eye, some nose details, some whiskers, and anything else you'd like to make your squirrel unique.

Fun Fact: A newborn squirrel is only about one inch long!

Did you know... According to an ancient Japanese legend, if you fold one thousand cranes you will be granted a wish. What do you think? Is this legend true? Why or why not?

See You Soon!

You made it to the end! Like all good things, this adventure must come to an end. But don't worry! There are many more adventures ahead of you. If you haven't already, maybe you'd like to join me for the adventure that started this series, my first book: *"Origami for Kids: Easy Japanese Origami Instruction Book for Kids."* There are all kinds of neat things in it that you can learn to fold!

We saw a lot of animals in this adventure. Did you also find any treasure while reading this book? What did you learn or discover as you made your way through? There are lots of fun and surprising facts about both animals and origami throughout this book. Did you get to read them all? I hope so! If not, take some time to go back and read a bit more. You may learn something really interesting, or discover something entirely new to you!

Maybe you discovered a true passion for origami. Maybe you found you love animal prints, or are interested in a specific kind of animal and would like to learn more about it. Maybe you simply discovered a love for reading and learning in a way you didn't know of before. Or maybe you had a good time, and now you're going to move on to a whole new experience. Whatever the case may be, I hope you enjoyed this journey!

You can make just about anything from paper. A paper cup, pretty gift boxes, wrappers, hopping frogs, coin purses, wallets, the options go on and on.

If you had fun and enjoyed yourself throughout this book, please let me know by leaving a review on Amazon. I'd love to hear your thoughts!

Thank you!

www.ingramcontent.com/pod-product-compliance
Lightning Source LLC
Chambersburg PA
CBHW070952080526
44587CB00015B/2279